Upon this Chessboard of Nights and Days:
Voices from Texas Death Row

Edited by
Dana Allen, Regina Bouley, Paula Khalaf,
James Ridgway, Haley Stoner, Daniel Stryker,
Cami Whitehead

Texas Review Press
Huntsville, Texas

FIRST EDITION, 2009

Requests for permission to reproduce material from this
work should be sent to:

> Permissions
> Texas Review Press
> English Department
> Sam Houston State University
> Huntsville, TX 77341-2146

Library of Congress Cataloging-in-Publication Data

Upon this chessboard of nights and days : voices from Texas
death row / edited by Dana Allen ... [et al.]. -- 1st ed.
   p. cm.
 ISBN-13: 978-1-933896-36-6 (pbk. : alk. paper)
 ISBN-10: 1-933896-36-1 (pbk. : alk. paper)
 1. Death row--Texas--Anecdotes. 2. Death row inmates--
Texas--Attitudes. 3. Death row inmates--Texas--Biography--
Anecdotes. 4. Prisoners' writings, American--Texas. I. Allen,
Dana, 1969-
 HV8699.U6T497 2009
 364.66092'2764--dc22
                                    2009024321

Publisher's Note

When my Editing/Publishing class met for the first time in the fall of 2008, I already had a topic ready for them: a chronicle of the plight of the churches of the Mississippi Coast in the aftermath of Hurrican Katrina. Since we had produced a highly successful book the year before on the history of the storm from its formation to its dissolution, this was a natural follow-up. My interns and I had been gathering material for the project for over six months.

Alas, not enough churches would cooperate, so three weeks into the semester, I declared the topic dead: There was no way we could produce a book thoroughly covering the impact of the storm on those churches without more thorough representation. Now we had to find a new topic and find it fast, so we set to discussing possibilities.

For some time I had been thinking about doing an anthology of prison writing, focusing on fiction and poetry, and I was especially interested in soliciting material from Death Row inmates. Who knew what talent lay among those men scheduled to die? I wanted to give them an opportunity to publish some of their work while they could. (This interest was a perverse outgrowth of a short story of mine, "Texas Death Row," which I wrote while I was teaching courses for Lee College in the old Ellis I, where Death Row was housed at the time.)

Gradually we fine-tuned our topic and decided that our book would be a compilation of art and nonfiction prose by inmates on Death Row. We wanted to know their dreams, hopes, fears, regrets; we wanted to know what it was like living in that place.

And here you have it: voices from "the Row."

This project belonged to my students, and they nursed it all the way from idea to finished product. I gave input when it was requested, but I gave them free rein to go wherever they wanted to with it. They put the book together, edited it, designed the cover, gave it the final proofing.

My gratitude to those hard-working students and to the inmates on Death Row who were willing to participate.

—Paul Ruffin

Table of Contents

Artwork

Upon this Chessboard of Nights and Days:
Voices from Texas Death Row

"But helpless Pieces
of the Game He plays
Upon this Chequer-board
of Nights and Days;
Hither and thither moves,
and checks, and slays,
And one by one
back in the Closet lays."

— Translated by Edward Fitzgerald
from Omar Khayyam's "Rubaiyat"

Orchestrating *Voices from*
Texas Death Row

The Texas Death Chamber, where the state of Texas carries out executions of more inmates than any other state in the nation, sits less than a mile away from where our graduate-level editing and publishing class meets each week. This death chamber is so near to Sam Houston State University that, in fact, there are actually some campus parking spots closer to the Walls Unit, where the death chamber is located, than to our classroom.

Yet, despite the proximity of the spot where anywhere from seventeen to forty men and women are put to death for capital crimes each year, Texas Death Row figures very little into the consciousness of those outside Huntsville's vast correctional system and the Department of Criminal Justice here at SHSU. Huntsville has no television stations that cover executions, so there is no major media coverage regarding Death Row except when particularly high-profile inmates are involved. Like most people in Huntsville, we go about our daily lives, hardly thinking twice about living blocks from the death chamber.

All that changed when Dr. Paul Ruffin, our professor, proposed the idea of putting together a book of nonfiction submissions from Death Row inmates. As we set out on this project, the Texas death chamber went from being an abstract thought to something tangible. Suddenly the 351 men and ten women living on Texas Death Row when we started in October 2008 went from nameless, faceless numbers to real people with real stories.

The purpose of this book is, simply, that we would like those on the outside to be aware of the humanity of those on the inside. We know that everyone who reads this will be coming into it with his or her own opinions regarding the death penalty, just as each of the editors involved in this project did. To this end, *Voices from Texas Death Row* was designed to be as unbiased as possible. Whatever our individual viewpoints or yours, the uniqueness of the stories in this book makes them worthy of being read, if for no other reason than to give readers an insider's view into a place that most of us will never know.

In our requests to Death Row inmates, we asked them to submit original artwork and nonfiction pieces about daily life on Death Row, the things that happen and the thoughts they have, along with memories from their past. Basically, we wanted them to share who they were in life before Death Row, what circumstances led them there, and who they are now as they wait for their execution date. Inmates were not paid for their submissions, and we reserved the right to edit them, which we did minimally, and mostly for the sake of clarity. Some inmates sent in biographical information on request, which we included, and others did not. We have also changed names of people whom inmates wrote about in their submissions to protect their anonymity. We felt it was important that we include input not only from the 350 men on Texas Death Row, but also from the ten women who are housed in a separate facility from the men. However, despite multiple requests to the female inmates, we received no responses. So the omission of female inmates here was not intentional—we would have loved to have highlighted their stories as well.

At first, we expected to receive stories primarily proclaiming innocence, but we were quickly proven presumptive when inmate submissions came pouring in. Yes, readers of this book will find tales within these pages in which an inmate expresses his claim of innocence, but *Voices from Texas Death Row* contains so much more. Some inmates take responsibility for the crimes that landed them on the Row and apologize to the families of victims or their own families left behind. Many discuss the role that their religious conversion in prison has taken in their lives, giving praise to God for changing their hearts. While some are passionate about perceived injustices, others are reflective about life on the Row and nostalgic about their former lives. Others offer humorous anecdotes that surprise readers who might expect darker stories from those behind bars.

Several included addresses in case readers wanted to contact them; to simplify this, here is the general address for the male inmates: [Inmate first and last name and inmate number], Polunsky Unit, 3872 FM 350, Livingston, Texas, 77351.

As we read through the submissions, we found ourselves surprised by the quality of writing that we received; many of the stories were so insightful and well-written that they shattered our preconceived notion that these inmates' submissions would need heavy editing for readability. The writing showed distinctive talents that are locked away in prison cells, and the intricacy and realism in the artwork submitted also showcase the range of skills on Death Row.

Impressed by what we read and saw, we then found ourselves shocked by the contrast of the perspectives from inmates and what we learned about the crimes for which they had been convicted. We intentionally chose not to mention details of these crimes so that readers of *Voices from Texas Death Row* could, like us, read the submissions at face value and not let the crime distract them from the content of the submission. However, readers who are interested in learning details of these crimes can visit the Texas Department of Criminal Justice website, www.tdcj.state.tx.us, to learn more about how the inmates ended up on Death Row. The juxtaposition of the submissions and the crimes the writers were charged with left us wishing time and again that the clarity expressed by many of the inmates today had been available to them earlier. Perhaps this could have altered the outcome of their lives and the lives of others.

It goes without saying that *Voices from Texas Death Row* would not have been possible without these inmates taking the time to share their stories, and we thank each one of them for their thoughtful contributions. We are also grateful to Dr. Paul Ruffin for his guidance in bringing to fruition a project that will have a lasting impact on each of us.

When we embarked on *Voices from Texas Death Row*, we never set out to change anyone's minds for or against the death penalty. Maybe you will finish this book and be angered, or saddened, or reflective. Maybe you will be further inspired in your own convictions, whatever they may be, or maybe your feelings will shift back and forth along the way. Maybe you will experience the entire gamut of emotions as you read these stories. Regardless, our hope is only that as you read them, you will take away something new by listening to these unheard voices before they, and the stories they relate, forever fade into the shadow of Texas Death Row.

—Texas Review Press staff

The views expressed in articles published in this book are those of the authors alone. They do not represent the views or opinions of Texas Review Press or its staff, nor do they represent the views or opinions of Sam Houston State University or any entity of, or affiliated with, the university.

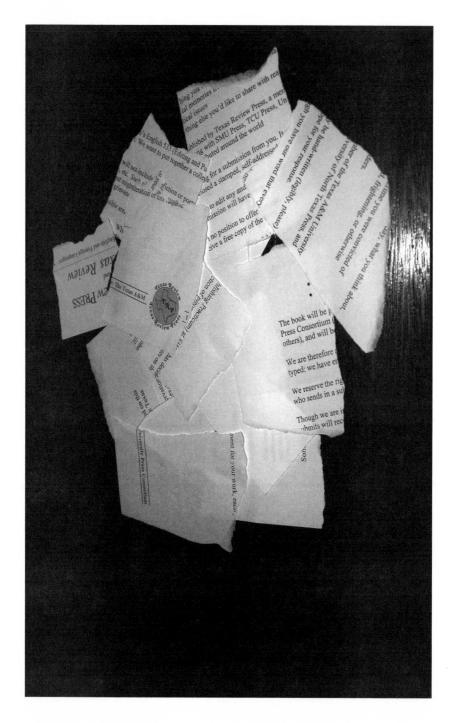

"No Comment" - Anonymous

Chronicling Capital Punishment in America's Busiest Death Chamber

The submissions from Texas Death Row inmates in this book present a unique glimpse into the cells and minds of those awaiting execution, but they do not present a comprehensive picture of the history of Texas Death Row. This introduction was compiled to provide clarity and background for the reader and to ultimately enhance the experience that comes from reading inmate submissions.

Demographics of Death in the Lone Star State

Of the thirty-seven U.S. states with death penalty statutes, Texas executes the most inmates annually, a record it has held every year since the U.S. Supreme Court officially reinstated the death penalty in 1976. In 2008, Texas sent eighteen Death Row inmates to Huntsville's execution chamber; Virginia ranked second highest that same year with just four executions. Over the past decade, Texas has executed an average of twenty-eight inmates each year, though at times that figure is considerably higher, as it was in 2000 when forty Texas inmates were executed.

As of this printing, 348 inmates sat on Texas Death Row, including ten females. This figure represents approximately ten percent of the total U.S. death penalty population; as of 2007, there were 3,220 people sentenced to death, with Texas, California, and Florida having the highest populations. On Texas Death Row, nearly forty percent of inmates are African American (39.1%), but close behind is an even mix of prisoners of Caucasian (30.5%) and Hispanic (29.3%) origin. The remaining one percent come from other racial backgrounds. Half of Texas Death Row inmates are under the age of twenty-five; however, the average age is thirty-nine.

From Hanging to Harnesses: The Origins and Evolution of Texas Death Row

Given its wild and often lawless past, it is not surprising that Texas leads the nation in inmate executions. Early on, the state was prowled by bears and wolves—and killers. Fugitives from justice called Texas home in its early days of colonization as a province of Mexico, then an independent nation, and then a U.S. state.

Until the third decade of the 20th century, hanging was the primary method of carrying out capital punishment in Texas. (One firing squad execution occurred during the Civil War.) Until 1924, authorities in the county were responsible for administering justice. However, a number of brutal county hangings moved the public to demand reform of the criminal justice system. Electrocution, which was thought to be more humane than hanging, was institutionalized in 1924, when capital punishment became the official responsibility of the State of Texas and a centralized Death Row was formed. The Walls Unit, so called because of the tall, imposing brick walls that surround it, was constructed in the southeast Texas town of Huntsville not long after the Civil War. Those sentenced to death after 1924 were placed on Death Row within the Walls Unit in a row of nine cells. The electric chair was the means of execution in Texas until 1977, when the state adopted a new method judged to be even more humane: lethal injection. This process involves strapping a prisoner to a gurney with harnesses and injecting him or her with a lethal combination of drugs that slow, then stop, the heart. The first execution by lethal injection in the United States took place in Texas in 1982.

Methods of execution were not the only aspects of Texas Death Row that underwent change in the 20th century. By the early 1960s, the state legislature and the Texas Department of Corrections moved to declare a moratorium on capital punishment. In 1964, Texas executed one last man in the electric chair; there would be no more executions in Texas again until 1984.

In 1972, almost eight years after Texas' self-imposed moratorium on capital punishment, the U.S. Supreme Court ruled in the case Furman v. Georgia that capital punishment was a "cruel and unusual punishment" that violated both the Eighth Amendment and the equal-protection clause of the Fourteenth Amendment. The governor of Texas cleared Death Row by 1973, commuting the death sentences of fifty-two inmates to life in prison. In 1976, the Supreme Court began to clarify specifics of the Furman case and allowed capital punishment with statutory guidance. Six years later, Texas used lethal injection to execute its first Death Row inmate since 1964. A more recent change, in 1996, declared that loved ones of victims should be allowed to witness executions.

The early part of the 20th century saw death sentences handed down in Texas not only for murder but also in some cases of rape, robbery, treason, counterfeiting, and arson. In 1973 the Texas Legislature passed House Bill 200, which limited capital offenses to those who had intentionally committed murder or were an accomplice to murder. In a murder trial, several questions have to be answered for the punishment of death to be rendered: Was the death caused intentionally and deliberately? Was the convicted person a continuing threat to society? Was the killing an unreasonable response to the provocation? An answer of yes to all three questions warrants a death penalty.

Today, the following crimes are considered capital murder offenses in Texas, according to the Texas Penal Code: murder of a public safety officer or firefighter; murder during the commission of kidnapping, burglary, robbery, aggravated sexual assault, arson, or obstruction or retaliation; murder for remuneration; murder during a prison escape; murder of a correctional employee; murder by a state prison inmate who is serving a life sentence for any of five offenses (murder, capital murder, aggravated kidnapping, aggravated sexual assault, or aggravated robbery); multiple murders; and murder of an individual under six years of age.

Capital punishment can also be sentenced through the Texas Law of Parties. While complex and difficult to summarize, basically this law states a person is criminally responsible whether an offense is committed by his own conduct or the conduct of another for whom he is criminally responsible. A person is criminally responsible for another if he helps another commit a crime, if he fails to attempt to prevent a crime he knows about, or if a separate felony is committed during the commission of another felony, even if there is no intent (i.e., a murder is committed during an armed robbery) because all participants should have anticipated the potential for additional criminal acts to occur.

In other words, many convicted under the Texas Law of Parties may claim the law is unfair because they may not have even been present at the crime but, due to surrounding circumstances and the language of the law, they were found guilty.

Life on Death Row

From the moratorium on the death penalty in 1964 until 1999, Death Row inmates were housed in the Ellis Unit, a correctional facility near Huntsville's death chamber. Since 1999, the male Death Row inmates have been housed near Livingston at the Polunsky Unit (once the Terrell Unit), which has the capacity to hold more than five hundred inmates. Women on Texas Death Row are currently housed at the Mountain View Unit in Gatesville.

While awaiting their sentence, Death Row inmates are housed in single-person cells, which measure approximately sixty square feet and have a non-glass window. Some are allowed radios and limited access to television, but inmates cannot control what comes on. Most inmates now spend their time reading, writing, and sleeping. They clean their own cells, receive a regular diet, and are recreated individually. They are confined to their cells for the vast portion of each day.

The average time an inmate spends on Texas Death Row prior to execution is just over ten years, though the longest is thirty-one years and the shortest only 248 days. The oldest inmate executed in Texas was sixty-six, and the youngest was twenty-four. One of the inmates whose story is included in this book, Jack Smith, is currently seventy-one years old, and his execution date remains unscheduled.

Prior to their execution, inmates are transported to the Walls Unit in Huntsville, where the death chamber is located.

Notorious Residents of Texas Death Row

Texas Death Row has seen its share of infamous inmates. Prior to the formation of an actual Death Row, the Walls Unit housed Kiowa Chief Santana and John Wesley Hardin, a gunfighter known as "the meanest man who ever lived," in the years following the Civil War. A member of the notorious "Bonnie and Clyde" gang, Raymond Hamilton, was housed on Texas Death Row. He escaped but was recaptured and executed in 1935 on a murder conviction.

More recently, national and international attention has turned to Texas Death Row over several high-profile inmates. Carla Faye Tucker, who was executed in 1998 for murder, became the second woman ever put to death in Texas and one of just three women executed in the 20th century in the United States. Tucker professed a conversion to Christianity while in prison, and many of the nation's prominent

Christian leaders appealed, in vain, for clemency from then-Governor George W. Bush.

The 2000 execution of another inmate, Gary Graham, brought not just worldwide media attention but political leaders and celebrities to the Walls Unit, along with protestors by the thousands. The Black Panthers and the Ku Klux Klan were also in attendance due to the controversy surrounding the case. Graham, who changed his name in prison to Shaka Sankofa, was sentenced to death for murder when he was eighteen, and prior to his execution eighteen years later, his innocence was heralded by Coretta Scott King, Bishop Desmond Tutu, the Rev. Al Sharpton, the Rev. Jesse Jackson, and celebrities Danny Glover, Kenny Rogers, Lionel Richie, and Harry Belafonte. The execution was witnessed by Jackson, Sharpton, and Bianca Jagger.

Only months after Graham's execution, the world turned its eyes to Texas again following the escape of a group of men who became known as the "Texas Seven." In December 2000, the men escaped from a prison in south Texas, stole guns and a vehicle, and murdered a police officer on Christmas Eve near Dallas. A nationwide manhunt followed, and a tip from a viewer of *America's Most Wanted* led to the arrests of the "Texas Seven" a month later in Colorado. All of the "Texas Seven" members received the death penalty, and one member of the "Texas Seven," Randy Halprin, submitted a story from his childhood for this book.

Just this year, the internet was abuzz with bizarre news of Andre Thomas, a Texas Death Row inmate who removed his own eyeball and ate it while in his cell. What makes this case more peculiar is that the man had already been partially blind from doing the same thing years earlier. Thomas has been declared sane under Texas law.

Is the Death Penalty on Life Support?

Nationwide, public support for capital punishment seems to be in decline. In 2007, New Jersey became the first state in four decades to abolish capital punishment, and the Supreme Courts of two other states declared capital punishment unconstitutional. Two years later, New Mexico's governor abolished the death penalty in his state. There is growing reservation about the death penalty regarding issues like unprecedented exonerations, DNA evidence, challenges to lethal injections, and questions over the arbitrariness of the death penalty.

Texans traditionally tend to support the death penalty in

higher numbers than the rest of the country, but even that margin is narrowing. A 2007 Gallup poll found that 69 percent of Americans supported the death penalty. The Texas Crime Poll, conducted the same year by Sam Houston State University in Huntsville, showed 74 percent of Texans in favor of capital punishment, a drop from 80 percent six years earlier. Public sentiment in Texas has a direct influence on capital punishment since appellate judges in Texas, who hand down sentences, are elected, not appointed.

Whether Texas will eventually follow suit with the much of the arest of the country regarding the death penalty is unknown. History has shown capital punishment abolished before, in many times and places, including Texas, only to resurface at a future date. While there is no way to determine whether or when the pendulum will swing back, one thing is known for certain: the matter of death weighs heavy on the minds of those who spend their nights and days waiting and wondering on Texas Death Row.

Works Consulted

"Crime Poll: Texans Have Less Confidence in CJ System." *SHSU Campus News Online.* May 2007 Sam Houston State University. 6 March 2009 <http://www.shsu.edu/~pin_www/T@S/2007/crimepoll07.html>.

Culp, Paul, director of the Thomason Room at the Newton Gresham Library at Sam Houston State University. Personal interview. 20 November 2008.

"Death Penalty." *Gallup Poll Online.* Oct. 2008 Gallup Politics and Government. 6 March 2009 <http://www.gallup.com/poll/1606/Death-Penalty.aspx>.

"Death Row Information." *Texas Department of Criminal Justice.* 5 March 2009 <http://www.tdcj.state.tx.us/stat/deathrow.htm>.

"Death Row Facts." *Texas Department of Criminal Justice.* March 2007. 5 March 2009 <http://www.tdcj.state.us/stat/drowfacts.htm>.

Donovan, Suzanne. "Shadow Figures: A Portrait of Life on Death Row." *Mother Jones.* July 1997. 25 Nov 2008 <http://www.

motherjones.com/politics/1997/07/shadow-figures-portrait-life-texas-death-row?page=2>.

Guthrie, Keith. *The Legend of Chipita: The Only Woman Hanged in Texas*. Austin: Eakin Press, 1990.

"Introduction." *Tarlton Law Library*. Oct. 2008 Jamail Center for Legal Research, U of Texas School of Law. 2 Nov 2008 <http://tarlton.law.utexas.edu/vlibrary/outlines/deathpenprint.html>.

Jackson, Bruce, and Diane Christian. *Death Row*. Toronto: Fitzhenry & Whiteside, 1987.

Longmire, Dennis, professor of criminal justice at Sam Houston State University. Telephone interview. 14 November 2008.

Marquart, James W. *The Rope, The Chair, And The Needle: Capital Punishment in Texas 1923-1990*. Austin: U of Texas P, 1994.

Murphy, Bill. "Death Row Status Quo." *Houston Chronicle*. 17 Sept 2003, A16.

Otero, Ana. "Supreme Court Preview: The Death Penalty in Texas." *American Constitution Society for Law and Policy*. April 2007. 6 March 2009. <http://www.acsblog.org/bill-of-rights-supreme-court-preview-the-death-penalty-in-texas.html>.

Texas Penal Code. Capital Murder. Stat. Sec. 19.03. 5 March 2009 <http://tlo2.tlc.state.tx.us/statutes/docs/PE/content/htm/pe.005.00.000019.00.htm>.

United States. Dept. of Justice. Capital Punishment Statistics. Washington: Bureau of Justice Statistics. 5 March 2009 <http://ojp.usdoj.gov/bjs/cp.htm>.

John Adams
#999278

Age: 46
Education: Ninth grade

My Story

My name is John and this is my story. At the young age of two my real mom gave me to a woman who I grew up believing was my mom until I was nine years old. I had everything a little boy could want: my family had their own business, the biggest plumbing company in Kenner, Louisiana. Then one night my "foster mom" called me into her room and told me they weren't my real parents. Do you know what this did to me? I hurt to no end and we both cried for hours. That day is still in my mind because from that point on, my life went downhill.

My last name as you see is Adams, yet my birth name is St. John. I'll tell you more about that later. What took place next? I was taken to my real mother's house and dropped off like a bag of clothes. When I went into the den, there were approximately ten to twelve people hanging out. My first thought was, "What is really going on?" Now understand here that the family that was raising me was Christian. I had not been around beer and such. Boy was I in for a big one here! All the people here were drinking and having a good time and there I sat, lost at nine years old. I met my big sister who took me by the hand and led me into the living room to get me away from all the noise. She became my sister and mom rolled into one. I love her with all my heart!

Well, after two years this man came to pick up my brother and sister. My brother and I had gotten real tight so I told mom, "Hey, I want to go!" So, off I went again. Just to find out that he was a drunk and that is when I started running the streets and doing whatever. At the age of fourteen, I left home, got a job at Shoney's and got into my own apartment with the help of [name withheld]. That is when I started drinking and smoking pot. That is when I thought, "Man, this is too cool." This continued on and life became even harder. At seventeen I ran off with a twenty-eight year old friend to Cincinnati, Ohio for work. By this time I was in my late teens and thinking I was ALL that! This was in 1979 so I had been on my own for two years. Things didn't work out there in Ohio. My friend left and I was homeless, so what did I do? I got my real mother to sign the papers and I joined the Army.

I was still drinking and now was stealing anything that wasn't bolted down. Does that sound like YOU? Even the Army couldn't break me. I stole $250 in cashier checks and a boom box, then decided to go AWOL. I didn't like being told what to do but of course the Army caught me. I received a write up and another chance. And what did I do? I blew it. I was drinking and doing drugs one night, and while I was on a date at the club, a guy started talking trash to the girl and myself. He pulled a knife so I pulled out mine and I proceeded to use mine to cut him up. After which I was sent to the stockade for thirty days, then I was finally kicked out.

At this point I turned to harder drugs, running the streets again, stealing, robbing and lying to my friends. I turned into a no-good human being. I was what most would call "white trash." By the time I turned twenty years old, I had worked a short time off-shore making good money just to return back to the streets. I hitchhiked and ended up in El Paso, Texas. That is where I had a few firsts: the first time I shot dope and the first time I had a run-in with the police. I got busted with rock cocaine. When I was in jail I was called down to be told that I was being charged with armed robbery. I had robbed a service station earlier with a friend. Yep, they got me and I received three years in Texas Department of Corrections and that, my friend, is where things fell apart.

As you can see I had gone from a little boy with everything into a young man with nothing yet I did have someone. That someone is my sister. She has stuck with me through this all. God bless her! To this day I love her even more for believing in me when I did not believe in myself.

While in Texas Department of Corrections I thought I had found my family, the Aryan Brotherhood of Texas. From 1985 to 2001, I gave them everything I had between the times I returned to prison five times. This time now is my sixth and my last, either way!

I gained the rank of Captain with this family, which took years. Yet through all these years God was talking to me. Had I listened, I might not be here today. I lived the life of a gang member, a biker, liar, thief, drunk and a dope head. But, it was my CHOICE to do what I did, just like it was my CHOICE to change my life. Jesus died on the cross for my sins and yours.

Now let me tell you how I started walking with God. I had been on death row for six years and my life was up and down. Three times I had written my lawyers and wanted to drop my appeals because I was so miserable. I was sent to level three and there you live in a seven foot by ten foot cell in which I behaved really bad.

One day a free world chaplain came there to visit a guy I knew very well, who explained to the chaplain that I needed to see him. I had never told him that but I'm glad that he did because this is the day that God started working in my life. Three months later I made Level 1, where I was around people again who didn't believe in God so again things got bad for me. There was one day that I was in the day room and there came the chaplain to see me. We shook hands and before I knew it he shouted "Jesus" at the top of his lungs. Boy you should have heard that section get quiet! I asked him why he did that. He said the Holy Spirit told him to. I looked at him and it was then I knew God was telling me, "Son, it's time to come to your real family."

That was when I gave my life to God, January 5, 2005 and I'm still walking with my Father. Two months later I heard on the intercom for me to pack my bags. I was being moved! The chaplain had mentioned a brother in Christ, a real good man who could help me with my faith. When I moved into his section, I was so happy. The next day in the day room I saw him and I shared with him what God was doing in my life and that I was changing my life. He had heard that statement so many times before but he said to himself, "Let's see what kind of fruit you show." Well sure enough I'm still here and have been following my brother's every move. He is my best friend and my brother in Christ. God put us together for a reason and only he knows what is going to happen. We are here for anyone who wants to give their life to God. We bear fruit and let our little light shine. God is so awesome! So my friend, it's your choice, "What are you going to choose?" Life or Death? I might be on the row but I am alive and I am FREE! FREE! FREE! May God bless you all and may he be your light (Romans 8:31).

God bless you all in the sweetest name ever, Jesus Christ, Brother John

Anonymous

Just thought I would send your envelope back!

I hate to see good money wasted for nothing.

Why is it everyone wants to make money off of us here on death row? Books, stories, artwork . . . and yet we cannot get help in fighting our cases! Cannot even get help with purchasing stamps or toiletries! Sad, don't you think?

Go ahead and write your stories, publish your books about us on death row . . . how is that going to help us? "Oh, it won't!" but I get a copy?

Yeah, I kind of thought you would laugh!

A Death Row Inmate

[Editors' Note: Any money made on this book will go into the TRP general fund, where it will be used to fund more books. Ours is a non-profit organization.]

Perry Austin
#999410

Age: *49*
Hometown: *None (born in Tacoma, Washington)*
Last school: *Central Texas College (while in prison on the Hughes Unit in Gatesville, Texas)*
Education: *GED, some college, various vocational trades*
Interests: *Dungeons and Dragons, reading, lots of different types of puzzles, some artwork*
Favorites: *I like a wide variety of reading material, although not too much on westerns and romances. Mostly horror, like Stephen King, but the best book I ever read was entitled* The Secret Life of Bees *by Sue Monk Kidd; it was really great. I'm not into cars, I like all ice cream, and I don't really like television. We don't have them back here anyway.*

My Dad was career military in the army so I never really had a real hometown. I was born in Tacoma, Washington where my Dad was stationed at Fort Lewis. I guess the closest thing to a hometown would be Cicero, Indiana where my Dad grew up and most of my kin on my Dad's side live. I never met or knew any of my kin on my mom's side. She's Japanese and her folks pretty much disowned her because she married my Dad. He's white. Because my Dad was in the army, we moved around a whole lot, never staying in one place more than a year usually. I lived in Munich, Germany for two years though during part of my first and second grades. Whenever my Dad had to go to Vietnam or was temporarily assigned somewhere he couldn't take us, we would all be left in Cicero until he returned, usually about a year. Cicero back in the early and mid-'60s was very small, around 1,900 people. Think Mayberry only smaller. We didn't have a junior high or high school, we didn't have a police station or town hall, or anything like that. We didn't even have a stop light. The main highway through "downtown" was a two-lane FM four-way stop. It was a town where everyone knew everyone.

My uncle was the town barber and just like you saw in Mayberry, it was where the town locals hung out to talk and play checkers. We had one town cop whose brother was the county sheriff. My grandfather was a dispatcher for the sheriff's department. Cicero was also a very, very racist town. There were no blacks or other families of color living within the town limits; there were no people of color in our elementary school or the junior high and high school in the next towns over. When the people of Cicero found out that my Dad had married a foreigner, the entire town was outraged. Because he was a hometown boy though it was pretty much accepted eventually. While it was "tolerated" by the adults, to a certain point, the other town kids were under no such restraints. I was very small for my size, and because of my race I was bullied unmercifully, most of which was overlooked by the adults. I was never allowed in the very few friends' homes I did have. When I started doing drugs and got in trouble, even these few friends were not allowed to play with me and so I spent a lot of my childhood by myself, wandering and exploring the vast woods around Cicero and the lake there. I think about Cicero and my childhood there a lot. It was a place that I hated because of what I experienced there, but at the same time I also miss it. I had some really good memories of the winters there, the exploring I did, etc. Anyway, it's changed; it grew.

I'll change the subject as I don't really talk about my family much. How do I occupy my time in here? Well right now I pretty much just sleep and listen to my radio or read my many D&D books and build one hundredth level characters! We've been locked down since October 13. We usually get locked down for a couple of weeks twice a year for a major shakedown. On October 13 we were locked down for that purpose but then some guy back here on death row got caught with a cell phone making threatening phone calls to Senator Whitmire. So Governor Perry ordered a statewide lockdown and search of every Texas prison unit and that's where we've been since.

We're not allowed to order books while on lockdown and the unit library is closed so I have nothing to read, except my D&D books and some magazine subscriptions that I have. I have a radio that I purchased from the unit commissary and I listen to it a lot when reception is good. We do not have televisions back here.

A typical day during lockdown would be I get up around 3:30 or 4:30 a.m. when they pass out breakfast johnnies. This morning's breakfast johnnie consisted of a squished piece of coffee cake and a peanut butter and jelly sandwich and a half pint of milk. I'll then wash up, wash my floor, and then try and catch the news on National Public Radio or one of the local radio stations. Around 9 a.m. I'll either break out my D&D books or nap until lunch johnnies. Lunch johnnies usually consist of two sandwiches, one of which is always a peanut butter and jelly sandwich. We get peanut butter and jelly sandwiches for every meal while on lockdown. Supper johnnies are pretty much the same as breakfast and lunch. After lunch it's pretty much the same thing again, take a nap or read my D&D books. If I've got letters to answer then I'll answer them.

When not on lockdown I will usually get up around 2:30 a.m. or 3 a.m. when they feed breakfast, clean up and wash my floor, listen to the news, then go to recreation where I'll do some exercises or talk to the guys in the cells surrounding the dayroom. The rest of the day is spent pretty much the same, reading, sometimes drawing, listening to the radio, writing letters. For a while I tried to engage in some educational programs, trying to self-teach myself Greek and German from work-study books I had ordered but, with the noise level in here and the constant interruptions, it was almost impossible to concentrate. Sometimes it's so loud back here that you can't even think straight.

Usually, when we're on lockdown for major shakedowns, we are still allowed to receive visits. Not this time though. Because the governor ordered the lockdown, all visits have also been suspended except for attorney visits.

I've been in prison pretty much my entire adult life. I was first locked up in jail in October of 1978 for a horrendous crime I committed against my family. I do not talk about it though. I was given a thirty-year sentence and spent the next thirteen years in prison on various units around Texas. I got out of prison on mandatory supervision, which is a type of parole, in September of 1991. While out I was doing pretty good, I had a job, my own apartment, my own car. I didn't have a driver's license or insurance or even the registration to the car. I had spent too long in prison that I didn't know how to do those things anymore and didn't know how to talk to people. The woman I first dated after I got out of prison, a co-worker at the bakery, helped me get my apartment.

Here is an example of how unprepared I was for society when I got out in 1991. A friend of mine met me at the Walls Unit in Huntsville to drive me to the halfway house in Houston. He knew that I loved McDonald's and so stopped off at one to get something to eat. I was so shocked at what I saw that I was literally unable to order. I just kept staring and staring at everything and the girl at the counter had to ask several times if she could help me before my friend made excuses for me and ordered something for me. So much had changed in thirteen years.

Anyway, I was doing well and dating one of my co-workers. She was married though and went back to her husband but she introduced me to her daughter. I started dating her daughter but there was just one problem with that. She was underage. At first it could have been excusable because I didn't know how old she was as I was introduced to her at the bar the woman and I hung out at. A couple of weeks later though I did find out and instead of dropping her like a hot potato, I continued seeing her. During the investigation of the offense of which I'm currently on death row for I was asked about my relationship with this girl and readily admitted it. I was subsequently arrested for this and sent back to prison with another thirty-year sentence. While in prison this time I got into an altercation with another inmate and ended up stabbing him several times.

For that I was placed in segregation for three years and got another twenty years stacked on top of my thirty. After getting out of segregation and transferred to another unit I managed to do pretty good but then got into an altercation with a prison guard. I was locked up and pretty much figured that I was going back to segregation and never getting out so I wrote a letter confessing to the murder that I am on death row for. My jury selection lasted two and a half days and the entire trial lasted two and a half days. I had no attorney as I elected to represent myself. I was determined to commit what the judge called "suicide by state." I questioned no juror and accepted whatever juror the prosecutor wanted to strike or keep. During the trial I called no witnesses nor questioned any. I spent most of those two and a half days eating candy and doodling on a legal pad. Direct appeals are mandatory so I had no choice there but I again elected to represent myself and while there did not file any motions or briefs, nor any writs. In June of 2003 I was finally given an execution date of September 8, 2003.

It was the week before my execution date when this woman I had met and my Dad convinced me to pick up my appeals. I've got some really good attorneys and they say that I have a good chance of getting off death row because I had made a false confession and because of my longstanding mental issues. They even told me that

I had a good chance of getting out of prison because although it is against the law to have relations with an underage girl, the girl and her mother have admitted that I had been deceived. But, the thing is, I don't want to get out of prison. This life is all I've known for thirty years. I know that sounds sad to some people but that's reality. I joke sometimes with the guys and my attorneys that if a tornado or hurricane ever knocked down the walls and fence of the prison unit, I wouldn't run. I'd stay right where I'm at. If the winds should pick me up and deposit me off out in the woods on the other side of the fence, I'd walk right back to the unit. The truth is though, I'd do exactly that. Come right back here and stay. I wouldn't know how to function out in the free world.

My attorneys and the friends I've made are always telling me that my current situation I'm in, my past difficulties, the people I've hurt, the family I've destroyed, none of it's my fault. It's because of my childhood and drugs and my mental health issues. These are good people and they really mean well and I really love them to death but, I do not and have never agreed with them on this. Sure I have mental health issues and sure I had a terrible childhood with bullying and other abuse. But, I was the one that chose to start doing drugs because I wanted to be "accepted" by the only group of people that didn't care what race I was. I was the one that chose to continue to do drugs even knowing what they did to me. How my entire personality changed. Everything I've done in my life, it was by my choice. Whether my choices were influenced by drugs or upbringing is irrelevant in my opinion. I used to blame everyone else for my troubles, especially my sisters and my Dad when I was younger. To me they were the cause of everything that went wrong in my life. I don't think that way now of course but it's a bit too late. I've already done the damage that can never be repaired.

When I first came to Death Row, I was an angry and bitter man. I was actively seeking my execution through non-participation of the appeals process. I had no attorney back then, electing to represent myself in order to speed up the process without interference. I kept to myself, didn't go to recreation, and shunned most conversation. I spent my days in my cell reading what I could get a hold of, listening to my radio, or staring out the widow. My first summer here was a dark and lonely one but I found joy in the littlest things, and also sadness. There was a wasp's nest being built right outside my window and I used to watch them build that nest every day, spending hours up at the window watching. I was devastated when the nest was destroyed. Shortly afterwards, I wrote this little piece and sent it into this newsletter called *HumanWrites*, a penpal organization that provides penpals for guys here on Death Row.

From My Window

Last summer I was watching these paper wasps building a nest right in the upper outside ledge of my window. It started out with just one wasp and I watched it build the main stem, then start making the little tubes. It would lay a little white egg-looking thing in it. I used to watch it every day.

Soon there were several tubes with eggs in it and I noticed that the eggs were growing and moving! As the nest got bigger the original wasp was joined by another.

Together they extended it, adding more tubes and more eggs. Then there were three. The nest was right up next to the window, so by standing on my rolled-up mattress I could see all of them real good. Sometimes one of them would stop working and, while hanging onto the nest with its back legs, it would stretch out towards the window and look back at me and sometimes try and touch my fingers whenever I put them against the window.

They became used to me standing at the window watching them and it was like, I don't know, we became friends. They were always well aware of me and one of them would always stop working and stretch out its front legs to touch the window every time I popped up there. I came to know and recognize every individual wasp. The black and yellow bands around their abdomens are just like fingerprints. They're all different. I used to spend hours every day watching them.

Then one day tragedy struck. The inmate paint squads were painting the cell numbers outside our windows and their scaffold knocked the nest off and destroyed it. I actually became quite depressed for a while and would often jump up on my mattress to look, hoping they'd try and make another nest. But they didn't.

It was probably too late in the year.

I was eventually persuaded to pick up my appeals by a woman I met through one of the penpal organizations and started writing more people, participating in more activities like recreation in here and writing things for newsletters outside. One newsletter asked us to write each month on various topics. One such topic was entitled "Simple Pleasures" and I decided that this was something I could write about.

Simple Pleasures

There is a common saying that goes something like this: "You don't know what you are missing until you've lost it." I think this is especially true for most of us in here. The simple pleasures that most people enjoy and take for granted (I'm guilty of the same) suddenly become painfully clear and missing from our lives when we come to prison. Simple pleasures:

—To be able to shower, use the restroom, take care of other personal matters in private without being observed and/or interrupted.

—To eat a meal that is not dried out and ice cold, or dried out and burnt to a crisp. A meal that tastes like something other than cardboard.

—To wear clothes that are clean and don't smell like they've been stuffed in someone's gym locker for the past few weeks. To not have to worry about whether we'll pick up a hitchhiker like scabies or staph.

—To be able to see the sky without having to look through a little slit in the wall and without the rolls of razor wire and fencing.

—To breathe in clean air and feel the wind and rain on your face.

—To see nature going on all around you. The squirrels playing and foraging for food, the wasps building their nests, the birds raising their chicks.

—To hear the sound of children laughing and playing in the distance and seeing other people going about their daily routines.

—And most of all, to feel the touch of another human in kindness, to see a friendly smile and hear warm words of love from family and friends. To be secure in the knowledge that you are loved and cared for. To have someone share the fears and doubts you have, to help chase them away and tell you that everything will be all right.

Some folks just don't know what they're missing until they've lost it all . . . the simple pleasures.

After writing this piece there was another topic entitled "Fresh Air." Fresh air is something that everyone takes for granted and never really thinks about. I know it was something I never thought about until I got back here. Even when I was out in population I never thought about it because we had windows everywhere that we could open and there was more open space, better air circulation.

Fresh Air

You know, I'm willing to bet that most people never give a second thought to the air they breathe while they go about their daily business. Unless of course something "unusual" happens to catch a hold of their olfactory senses, say the odor of a skunk. But I think there's one group of people who are unusually all too aware of the air they breathe, prisoners who live in an enclosed environment. I live in such an environment. Texas Death Row.

On Death Row we don't have windows in our cells that we can open to get a whiff of that fresh air. We have what they call an "air-cooling" system. Is it an air conditioner? Whatever it is, it sure is great at cooling the air in here during the winter months! It's not so efficient during the summer months though. When it is working, the air in the cell sometimes has a metallic or burned wire smell. That's preferable to what's outside the cell door though!

I keep my fan pointed towards the door of my cell, so that usually keeps the more obnoxious smells out. But once I step outside my cell, whether going to recreation, shower, or to a visit, the various odors assault the senses like a stampede of cattle. The main odors to assault your senses are the musty, sweaty smell of too many unwashed bodies enclosed in too small a space without proper air circulation. Then you have the rusty mildew smell from the showers, the rotten sour smell from the spilled food on the runs. Sometimes you'll catch a strong smell of feces or urine. On the disciplinary pods you have all of this and pepper spray thrown in for good measure. These smells are a constant in our lives and our senses soon acclimate themselves so that soon, you don't even notice it, until you leave to go to a visit that is.

Visitation is in another building and to get there you have to go outside. The first thing you notice when you step out is the air. It smells clean and fresh! You smell the grass, the flowers, the very air itself! You take a deep breath and hold it in. Then you breathe in some more as you slowly make your way to the visiting room, trying to prolong exposure to something most people take for granted and never think about. But you know this is something special and precious.

Two hours later (four, if it's a special visit), your visit is over and you make that return trip back to the building housing death row. Again you take your time, enjoying the pleasure of breathing in clean fresh air. Then you step into the building and the smells hit you like a West Texas thunderstorm, violently assaulting your senses. It is the smell of human misery and despair. You crinkle your nose and grit your teeth and shuffle your way back to the pit you call home.

A sweet, rotten, sour smell is emanating from the small kitchen off the main hallway. Gee, I hope that isn't our dinner!

When I had an execution date and was placed on death watch with the other guys waiting to die, I noticed the many different ways the guys back there coped with the knowledge that chances were likely that they were soon to be dead and gone from this world and gone from life as they know it. Some guys kept their hopes alive that they would get a reprieve, that they would get that last minute phone call telling them that they got a stay. Other guys had their faith in whatever god they believed in and prayed. Some guys acted indifferent and went about their daily activities as if nothing unusual was happening. I sort of fell into this last category. It wasn't that I wasn't concerned. I had prepared myself for death. This was something that I had worked towards for the past couple of years when I decided to confess to this crime for which I am condemned. There wasn't so much fear of death as there were doubts about what came afterwards. Is there really a God? Was there really a heaven and hell? If so, which would I go to? Or, did we just suddenly cease to exist into nothingness? Then I picked up my appeals, and while the doubts and questions lingered, there was a different fear now, different doubts and worries. The doubts and worries and pressures that come from living. It was while thinking about all of this that I wrote this thing on "Courage" and what it means. To me anyway.

Courage

Some say that to know the exact time and date of one's death and yet still be able to walk calmly towards it with head held high takes an extraordinary amount of courage. In a state where the assembly line of death has speeded up while other states have slowed down or put theirs on hold, where the state legislature and judicial system and the majority of its citizens are so rabidly pro-death penalty, most of us know deep down that the chances of a reprieve are very, very slim. That we too will eventually take that final short walk to the gurney and face what everyone in this world will one day face in the end.

The constant specter of death hovers over us all here on death row, day after day, week after week, month after month, year after year. Yet the men and women on death row continue to fight, continue to hope, continue to live for another day.

Some say courage is the ability to face death calmly, or without fear. But to me, it takes more courage to live. Courage to wake up each day with the certainty of knowing that nothing has changed, that your future holds nothing but more pain and heartache, more loneliness. Courage to wake up each day knowing that even though you are surrounded by life, by hundreds of other human beings, you are still alone with yourself, alone with your past. For me, death would be a welcome relief from the daily gut-wrenching pain of despair and hopelessness. A simple step. But do I have the courage to take that step? No.

While listening to my radio I sometimes hear news reports on upcoming or just past executions and often hear the families of the victims or victims rights groups express anger and frustration that the guys back here are still living and breathing while their loved ones are dead and how the appeals process takes so long, how we'll sit back here for years sometimes. When I hear that I sometimes think, "If they only knew."

If they only knew how each day back here is a sort of living hell. Just imagine living in a little concrete box that's no bigger than your walk-in closet. Your commode and sink just a few feet from your bunk. Your daily activities regulated constantly. The total, complete lack of privacy for even the most personal of bodily functions. The amount of possessions you own able to fit into a small two cubic foot box, and even then is subject to confiscation for whatever reason. The horrible food you're fed day after day. It never changes, it never varies. Your life subject to the whim of whoever happens to be working the pod that day. Allowed out of your cell once a day for two hours, five days a week into a dayroom that's just another, bigger version of your cell with a table and pull-up bar. The never-ending days of boredom and monotony, nothing to do but whatever you can come up with, or days spent thinking about your life, where you come from and where you're going. A life in here knowing that this is it, that this is all you've got to look forward to for the rest of your life. More of the same.

I've only been on death row for about six and a half years and I've seen guys come in here seemingly without a care in the world, only to break several years down the line from the isolation and monotony. Withdrawn and haggard, isolating themselves further from everyone. I've seen guys unable to take the stress and isolation anymore and commit suicide. A lot of people don't realize how bad life back here is and how once we're dead, our suffering is over. Some might ask if life is so bad back here and death would be an end to suffering, why do guys continue to fight, continue with their appeals? Because it's human nature to want to continue living. Even if it's only instinctively.

Sincerely,
Perry A. Austin

Rigoberto Avila, Jr.
#999391

Age: 36
Hometown: El Paso, Texas
Last school: J. M. Hanks High School, El Paso, Texas
Education: Twelfth grade
Interests: Spending time with my son and family and baseball
Favorites: Book - Beyond Belief *by Josh Hamilton; Movie* - Blood In Blood Out*; Ice cream - pistachio almond; Car - Chevy Camaro*

Can't Keep a Good Man Down

On April 30, 2001, I was convicted of the murder of a nineteen-month-old boy. I can honestly admit that I'm innocent of this crime. I want to take this opportunity to make you, the reader, aware of a situation not to get yourself into, so that hopefully you won't fall into the trap that I did.

The evening of February 29, 2000 I was asked by a friend if I would babysit her two kids and her other son who was three years old. I accepted, being that I had done so numerous times before. Afterwards, she was acting very strange in such a hurry to leave her apartment so she could attend her evening class. Well I didn't think much of it, which I should have. Before she left her apartment she came out of her bedroom and that's when I asked her where was [name withheld]. She replied to me, "if you say anything about what happened I'll have your mom killed." At that moment my whole life changed because I knew I wasn't going to let anything happen to my Mom. As a result I took the fall for a crime she committed in which I was set up by her.

My motto has always been, "you can't keep a good man down" and to this very day I remain very hopeful that one day I'll be exonerated of this crime.

Respectfully submitted,
Rigoberto Avila, Jr.

Danny Bible
#999455

Age: 57
Education: Twelfth grade

The First Amendment is the very key to the doorway of the Bill of Rights. That is why it is the first before all the others. It is backed by the very charter that we hold so dear to our freedoms. Which blood stained parchment is our rock and final bastion to all rights fought for and which preserves for a free nation its rights when it keeps an eye out for unjustice of any kind even against the power of just the one. Amend or abridge this right and the gate is closed, and unjustice will rule by the unselect few in their own unjustice called justice for all but us.

When the rights of just the power of one person are denied, because they are only just the power of one, wouldn't all the powers of one denied fill an ocean of denial for us all? The First Amendment is not just a key for the press but for all the people who wish to speak or print their own grievances for all who want to hear or see it. An informed nation is a well prepared one, ready to fight for the rights of just the one who was denied their rights whatever they may be.

Lester Bower
#000764

Age: 60
Hometown: Arlington, Texas
Last school: Texas A&M University, College Station
Education: Four years college
Interests: Hunting, fishing, camping, flying
Favorites: It's tough to pick a favorite "anything" when you've been exposed to so little for so long.

True Story #1

I arrived on the row in 1984, but this story isn't directly about me. It's a story about a good friend of mine who arrived about a year after I did. I didn't meet him right off the bat, but I knew who he was. He went by the handle "Professor." Now almost everyone had a handle they went by, and he felt that since he had some time up at Stephen F. Austin being a Lumberjack, he was entitled to be called professor. I, on the other hand, had done my apprenticeship over in College Station where everyone in the state thought we spent all our time thinking up jokes. He (I never called him professor) and I finally met up, went over to the Work Program together, and even celled together for a time. During that time I had to listen to all the latest Aggie jokes, who knows how many times, most of which I had heard years ago. On one particular night after being subjected to another Pollack joke. I turned to my friend and said "I think I'll change your handle to BUBBA." I could tell from his reaction that he felt BUBBA was not to the high standards professor gave him, but there was also that glint of concern on his face.

During this same time frame I was recording a radio program out in the visitation room during media day. A reporter from a Houston paper came almost every Wednesday, and he would call me and anyone

I wanted out for a visit. He brought a small cassette recorder, which he would turn on right in front of where I would sit, and then he would go off and interview anyone he had scheduled. I, along with at least one guest, would talk about prison issues, especially Death Row issues, for about eight to eleven minutes, and then we would just wait till the reporter came around and turned off the machine. He then took the machine back to Houston with him, dropping it off with the producer of a prison program that aired on KPFT Radio Sunday afternoon called THE INSIDE MAN. On this particular day I had Bubba out with me, and on the air I called him Bubba several times. Well, the next week after the show aired everyone was calling him Bubba, and the more he begrudgingly protested, the longer they kept it up. After a while, no one remembered that his old handle had been professor. From then on everyone just called him Bubba.

One evening we were discussing his change of handle, and his continuing dislike of the aforementioned name. I thought about it for awhile and I knew he was watching me. Finally, I said, "Okay, we'll change your handle if you want. I think we should call you BUBBLES." He got that instant horror stricken look on his face, and then after a thoughtful pause he just said, "Well maybe Bubba isn't so bad after all." From that day on, for many years, he was just affectionately known as Bubba. You sometimes have to be careful who your good friends are when you live . . . on the Row.

True Story #2

When I first got to the Row in 1984 it seemed that almost everyone had some kind of pet. The Ellis Unit had a lot of critters running around, and some made their way to the inmate cells. There were small birds that were taken as chicks from roofs off the outside recreation yard, rats (which looked more like field mice to me), some lizards, a snake or two, but by far the most numerous pets were spiders. Death Row had one of the best collections of Black Widows I've ever seen. Needless to say there were some risks in keeping "The Widow," but I've never heard of any serious bites. One day a friend of mine was out in the yard, and by chance he came across a good size wolf spider which he gently coaxed into his peanut butter jar that he had taken from the yard to drink from, and brought it to his cell.

When evening shift came, we noticed the officer assigned inside the wing was one of those officers who were overly diligent in the pursuance of his job. We simply called it a pain in the ass. We wanted to "spread" that evening where someone makes some sandwiches and then we pass them up and down the run through the bars. This officer didn't believe we had the right to pass anything, whether it was a book, a newspaper, or even a sandwich or two. What we clearly needed was a plan, and it didn't take creative people very long.

At this time Texas Department of Criminal Justice allowed inmates to smoke, and they sold small boxes of wooden matches in the commissary. My friend with the wolf spider put on a pair of cotton gloves, emptied out one of those matchboxes, and gently folded the legs of the spider till he could fit into the matchbox. By this time it was dark out on the run, and what light there was came from the cells, and it lit up the floor out onto the run. Everyone had a "Giggers" mirror that they could stick through the bars to look down the run, and when the officer is looking the other way, the matchbox was sent out on the run, about six feet in front of the cell. Then, in a voice much too loud to be secretive, someone said "Hurry, get that back before he sees it. Come on hurry up." Of course I looked down the run, and he came after it at not quite a run, but more like a competitive speed walk where you shift your hips from one side to another as quickly as possible to cover as much ground as possible. He snatched up the matchbox, and just for good measure someone said "Oh no," ever so quietly, but not quietly enough. He had that triumphant smile on his face as he opened up the box to see what manner of contraband he had seized, and when the lid was open, I'm here to tell you, the wolf spider was getting somewhere. The color absolutely drained from the officer's face, which was noticeable even though it was dark out on the run, and his face color was already of a dark persuasion.

Now I won't say he screamed like a woman, as he tore down the run to the safety of the picket, but it did sound somewhat like the wail of a banshee. For the remainder of the night, he never left the top of the milk crate he was sitting on, and we managed to pass out the spread without further incident. Within thirty days we never saw that officer again.

It just takes a certain disposition to work . . . on the Row.

True Story #3

Beginning in the mid '80s, until it was discontinued in 1998, Texas Death Row had a Work Program, and a good proportion of the inmates worked at a meaningful job, most of which were out in a garment factory where they sewed officers' uniforms. No one ever thought it would work, but for over twelve years inmates walked around unrestrained, recreated in large groups and worked at a job without killing each other. Except for the DR on the clothes, you couldn't tell the difference between the Death Row Garment Factory and a General Population Garment Factory, and that was the downfall of the program. If these inmates were not a threat to commit violence to themselves and others, then why weren't they serving time in general population? That's another story altogether, so let's get back to this one.

When I first went out to the factory I worked on the floor sewing, just like anyone else, but eventually I worked my way into the position of office clerk. One day I was coming out of the offices at one end of the factory, going to check on a shipment in the other end. As I walked down the center walkway, I saw two inmates "jawing" at each other off to one side. Now, "jawing" isn't quite an argument, but a little more serious than a loud discussion. As the "jawing" got a little louder people started turning off their sewing machines to see how this was all going to play out. I'll call the two inmates Peanut and Little Joe (not their real names), and Little Joe's job was working on a sewing machine, and Peanut's job was cleanup. The "jawing" seems to have reached its end, and Little Joe had turned around to start sewing again. I started to walk on until I saw Peanut go back to the bathroom area and return with a commode brush. Now, down here we would not call it a commode brush, we would call it a Shitter Brush, and when new it would have been a formidable weapon. The brush was wooden, about eighteen inches long, and a handle one and a quarter inches in diameter.

Well, Peanut came up behind Little Joe and swung the brush around, hitting Little Joe in the shoulder or back area. I wouldn't say it was a crushing blow, but what you get is a sound you get when you take your index finger and thump a large Black Diamond watermelon to see how fresh it is. To Peanut's surprise and everyone else looking on, the brush just broke off and fell on the floor. Apparently the wooden handle had become so rotten that it didn't take much of a blow to break the head off. Little Joe showed very little reaction to the blow, and just turned around to Peanut and said "Well fool, what are you going to do now?" The factory was silent for what seemed like an eternity, but of course it was just a few seconds. Then, and I can't say to this day who, but someone began laughing, and it just became infectious until the whole factory was laughing, including Peanut and Little Joe. Little by little the laughter died down, men started up their machines to continue working, and Peanut picked up the brushhead, and when the handle broke he threw it away in the trash.

I learned later from another source that the "jawing" was over some coffee that Little Joe had borrowed from Peanut that he thought was being repaid a little too slow. It sure couldn't have been much of a problem, because later that night, I saw them out in the dayroom playing dominoes together. That was the only violent (if you want to call it that) act that happened in the factory in over twelve years of operation. For supposedly being around such violent people, after incidents like this, you sometimes have to pinch yourself and ask, "am I really living . . . on the Row?"

Anibal Canales, Jr.
#999366

Age: 46
Education: *Tenth grade*

HELP WANTED!!!

Are you human? Do you think of yourself as a compassionate person? When you look at your life, do you feel like it's not fully complete? Do the images of injustice strike you as deeply as they do your family and friends? Do you ever ask yourself, "is there more to life?" or "where is the activism in the world?" Have you ever driven by a stranded person and spent the day regretting your action? And wondering who they are or why they were stranded, and why you didn't help them in their time of need? Does the idea of your past make you nervous when thinking of your future? When someone mentions "Karma"? Has the thought of a Greater Purpose entered your mind? If you have answered "yes" to any of these questions, then I'm talking to you!! Why?? Because these same questions once plagued me. And I answered them all "yes" and because I did, I did something about it!!

I am a Death Row inmate in Texas. I was sentenced to die in November 2000. And since that time I have looked within myself. And asked questions I didn't have the courage to ask before. And I didn't like what I saw and the answers I gave myself. Truth hurts. I'm over forty. Been in prison all my adult life. And then some. Never been married. No kids. And nothing to show the world that I was even here. And to be perfectly honest, I wouldn't have been missed if they had killed me that very day that I was sentenced to die! Sad. But true. For the last seven years, I have come to some stark realizations about myself and my past. And the system that sentenced me to die. And the fact is that we were both broken. My soul and the justice system of this state and nation. We both need to heal and find closure to the chapters filled with pain, suffering, bloodshed and cruel punishment it has inflicted on others and itself. And to that end I have begun a spiritual journey. If you will to seek that closure to those dark chapters and with the help of my truly loving friends and family I have begun that process for myself and now I turn my attention to the justice system of Texas and the USA and in order to do that properly I need your help—hence the "Help Wanted."

I need people like you!! People who have asked the same questions that I have asked and seek to better themselves and their world community by actively becoming part of the solution rather than allowing the continuance of the problem!! You have the ability to help me. Help you. Help this system and find answers to the questions that we all ask ourselves and those around us. If you have the time, energy, and the commitment to become part of the positive activism that I'm working on then I want you to contact me!! I want to meet other human beings that care and who seek to attain the same goals that I do—which is: THE ABOLISHMENT OF THE DEATH PENALTY!

Thomas Payne said, "In order to be the best human that you can be, you must serve something greater than yourself"!! What service is greater than to fight for and save life—human life?? If you are willing to help me fight for my life, I want you in my life!! My time is precious to me, and I will not waste it playing games with it. I spent a greater part of my life doing just that and look where it got me. I am financially secure, in a loving and committed relationship. I have wonderful and inspirational friends that make my life worth living and guide me in my activism, so if you want to become part of this and part of my life and become a fellow fighter for life, then by all means contact me. I look forward to hearing from you and until then I send you my deepest respects and regards and wish peace and love on you and yours.

Shout Out!!

To my mother,

Shalom Mama. Today is the day is it not? Fifteen years . . . And I still remember it like it was yesterday. I came over to your house before work and brought you pizza and we had a couple of pops and a slice. You said you hadn't been feeling well. You even went to the hospital a couple of days before that. They told you that it was just migraines and gave you some pills. Anyhow, we sat there and [name withheld] came home and we talked and laughed some. I called work and told them I would be late. You wanted me to go to the store for you and pick up some stuff for [name withheld] when she came over for the weekend. As you walked across the living room and then sat down, and then laid down on the couch . . . and you looked at me and terror filled your eyes. And I knew . . . I knew. [Name withheld] called 911, and I sat there holding your hand and telling you that you would be all right. And as I did Mom, I held on to my own fear with both hands so that you wouldn't be scared. You smiled at me and mouthed I love you. And it was the last time that I saw your eyes filled with love and recognition of your only son.

I died that night, Mama. I died when I heard the doctor tell us, and I died every day since. That was in 1992, May of that year, that day plays in my mind every year. And it was in May of 1998, as I was passing through Beto One, back to Telford after getting out of the hospital for another small stroke. I was on X-wing, and heard the keys and when the pigs stopped at my cell door and said the chaplain wanted to see me. I knew again. I knew. As I heard [name withheld] tell me over the phone and had this stranger hold my shoulder as I died inside again. "Mom died last night, Andy." And there was this roaring in my ears. I went back to my cell holding onto my sanity and I heard this screaming. And it took me a moment to realize it was me.

And by the end of the night I came to two realizations. One, I failed you as a son, and two, my life had become meaningless and had for years when I failed to hear you and heed all the warnings that you had given me, and to this day, Mama, I am ashamed, because I know that you see me now, and know that I have again failed to heed your warnings. I have spent a lifetime in cells like this, and through it all, I knew that I had your love. I never understood what it meant until I grew up and knew it for what it was, and for that love, I thank you, Mom.

And I say this in front of many people, so that you know that I have finally come to terms with me, and now I know what you were talking about. Too late? Maybe. But until my time comes whether it's here on Death Row or I get a chance to hit that street one more time, I will make this vow to you—and you knew even then, when I gave my word, you could count on it—I will spend my life making you proud Mom, because one day I will face the Almighty, and you will be there along with many who will speak for me and those that will speak against me. And I want nothing more than to see your face shine with pride that your son has finally taken control of his life, and made something of it rather than destroying it. And you'll know that those ties that had so much control in my life have been cut and now I am master of my own fate.

Before I go, Mom, I want you to know a few things. I miss you and you are never far from my thoughts and always in my heart. I wish that we could talk and laugh, have a few beers and just chill, like we used to. I treasure those few years that I had out there with you. I'm always laughing at memories of us playing pool and listening to Ramon Ayala. Smile. [name withheld] graduates on Wednesday and I wish we both could be there. Well, it's time to go, Mom. But let me say thank you. For what? For so much but the one memory that I hold dearest in my heart is when you laid on that couch and mouthed, I love you, and I held your hand and told you that I love you too Mama. Shalom.

In memory of my mother and friend, May 29, 1998

The Revolution.........Within!!!

"In order to be a better human, you must serve something greater than yourself."—Thomas Payne, *Rights of Man*

You and a friend are sitting in front of a store and drinking a soda, and you watch a truck full of men pull up and drag a man out of the bed of the truck . . . and they pull him to the back of the store, to a tree, and begin to tie a rope around his neck. The man that is being held down is kicking and screaming for help. He is yelling and begging for you and your friend to help him. One of the men holding him turns and tells you, 'Stay back, this is state business." What do you do?? WHAT DO YOU DO??!! WHAT??!! What do you, as a human being that you say you are, DO??!!

I know what I would do, but I wonder what *you* would do . . . I see a group of men drag a cat out of a truck kicking and screaming, I go find out what the hell is going on, and if I don't like what I hear, then we got problems right then and there!! Simple as that, but that's me. What about you?

This scenario is not what happens every time an inmate is put to death here in Texas, no, no. This scenario is a man that really does not want to die. This is a man that believes in the goodness of his fellow human being no matter what he had done. He is screaming not only to protest the treatment that he has found himself under, but slow, he knows that if he doesn't, he may die without anyone knowing it. This is a man that wants someone to hear him die, to witness the murder that is about to happen in front of the world!! Yet here in Texas Death Row, and death houses across the United States, not a peep!!! I personally have been out there in the visiting room when three inmates are set to die, and at one time I was living in a cell where I could witness inmates leave for Huntsville from the back dock. And not once did I see a single inmate cry out for help, scream out his anger, plea for his life, or even curse the very people that are set to kill them. Not one time have I seen a man fight for his life . . . NOT ONE TIME!! Yet, I have seen all of them smile at their executioners, laugh, cut it up, joke with the very men and woman that will help strap him down in the gurney, and inject the poison in their arm!! The very same men that "claim" that they are innocent, meekly walk to their deaths.

Just last week, [name withheld] did the same. This woman "claimed" that she was innocent and swore that she didn't do this terrible crime, yet when it was time, she walked to her death without a peep. So, I ask you, what would you do?!! I am willing to bet that if you do what I do, and get out of the car and go and find out what is going on, ask questions, and make yourself find out why they are killing this man, you won't allow this to happen to you either—yet it does—many times a year, especially here in Texas. And I am willing to go further that if you had done all that and got involved whether to help the man or not, you would have went home that night, with the *knowledge* of a *human being* that you may or may not have helped, point is, you knew that man!! He was a human being that you saw die or helped save . . . his struggle and terror propelled you to get out of that car, put down the paper and soda, and get involved, either for him or against him. YOU were there!! And, no matter what, you have that human being engraved in your mind, you are home talking about that man, telling your family about it, seeing it on the news, and they are talking about him too, about his family, his past, the people that loved him or even hated him, he is no longer the nameless faceless number that he was when you woke up that morning. Regardless of his crime, his guilt or innocence, that human being is now on the minds of the citizens that allowed that man to die, to be MURDERED!!

Ladies and gentlemen, we are all guilty of this idea that it is courageous to WALK to your death, we see it on the TVs and the movies, the long walk down the hallway, the man with the stiff upper lip, the priest walking beside him saying, "Be strong" with his hand on your shoulder, back straight, with the echoes of the well wishes of the "condemned" friends still ringing in his ears. We are all guilty of listening to the "SPIRITUAL ADVISOR," telling us that we should have faith in God, that it's okay, that God will stand with us, that Jesus didn't fight the sentence that was imposed on him. And the warden comes to your door, and tells you it's your time, and asks you are you going to walk to it like a man, or do we have to carry you to it?!! We are all guilty of promoting this and giving weight to these very things—myself included!!

I can't say what will happen when it's my time. IF that times comes, I can say this though: I have made the decision not to go out like that!! I refuse to be killed without a face and a name! I refuse to die without showing the world that I deserved more than being dragged to my death. And brothers and sisters, THEY WILL DRAG ME AND FIGHT WITH ME ALL THE WAY TO THE GURNEY!! They will *know* that they are killing a human being!! And you should do the same. You ask why? Allow me to tell you, please.

By allowing yourself to be MURDERED without so much as a peep from you, gives them, THE MURDERERS, a clear conscience!! See, most people in this world equate guilt or innocence with the showing of emotion, something that gives them a handle on the effect of what's happening to them, or to you, even remorse is shown with more than indifference, and when you hop up on that gurney, and quietly speak your peace and say goodbye to your loved ones, and then turn to the victims' families. And tell them you're sorry or not, then they feel like they have done their "duty" and that it was done within the law, and they feel okay about it, they go home and maybe tell their families it went good and he didn't fight, so, he must have had this moment with God . . . and knew he was guilty.

And there is the *crux* of the matter!! They think that because you went to your death without a peep, and didn't give them any trouble, no fighting or anything, that you are guilty, and that you got what was coming to you!! And that *feeling* is what allows them to accept the MURDER of a human being! And that, brothers and sisters, is what we have to take away from them, that comfort that they feel!! Strip them down to their conscience!!!

By stepping forward and fighting for your life, knowing that there is no win, that you will be executed, because believe me, all the fight in the world isn't going to change the fact of your death, may seem pointless, but it's not!! It gives hopes to the next human being that must face that MURDER, it gives you a moment to scream out your frustration with a system that allows the senseless MURDER that is about to take place, with you as the honored guest, it allows you to fight for a justice that, *you know*, isn't forthcoming. It gives your family and loved ones and friends and supporters the strength to go on the march and in the trenches with you!!! To go out there in front of the death house and fight for the injustice that is taking place, just like you did for that man that was screaming and kicking when they dragged him behind the store! It shows the world that you are a human being, and that you are entitled to life!! And, barring *that*, then you are entitled to their undivided attention, and respect and that you are much more than the man that was convicted of these terrible crimes—MUCH MORE!!! Your guilt or innocence is irrelevant now, your life and the taking of it, is the matter at hand. And you, and only YOU, can wage this battle!!

We all have seen that the voices of the protestors and the sight of them outside the walls is of no account to the state. It barely registers with the local newspapers, media in general, not even a mention on the front page. But YOU, you can make them be heard. You can help further the cause, and show the world that this is no longer acceptable to us, as a people, as human beings!! It has to begin here in TEXAS, because our machine is a real one, with real teeth, and it's fueled on the blood of past executions, oiled with the indifference of the citizens that purchased the machine. We MUST make that machine misfire and lose momentum! We MUST force the citizens to see that the machine is no longer working quietly, and that the fodder that feeds the machine isn't going to the gallows, like cows to the slaughter, any longer! They must see that they have to spend some money, and time, and sweat, and shed some blood, now to kill a human being. IT AIN'T EASY NO MORE!! And WE are the only ones that can make that happen. WE ARE!!

Now, you're thinking, well, that's really easy to say, when you're living on another pod and not here on death watch, right? And you would be right, to an extent. I don't know your mindset. I don't know what you are about to go through, I don't know what fears you are facing. I can only draw from my experience and I have always found that this is true, no matter where I am, on death watch, general population, in the world. I have always, always ALWAYS!!, fought for my life, when that life was threatened!! No matter who it is, no matter if I win or lose or die, I will fight for mine!! I have NEVER paid for protection. I have never allowed another human being to sell me a hog. I have never allowed anyone to use or abuse me, and I have never allowed anyone to instill such fear in me that I would fold up and give up!! NEVER!! And I don't see that happening now. I have spent most of life locked up in Texas institutions, and not once did I ever go out like a sucker!! And, that's exactly what you would be doing if you allow the state or another human being to walk to your cell and tell you that he is going to kill you later today, and if you don't give them any trouble, then I will give you a good meal and let you walk to it like a man!!!!!

In other words, he doesn't think you're a man or woman anyhow, but for the sake of getting you to the gurney without any trouble, he will LET you think you're a man or woman for one day!!

Brothers and sisters, you don't need this state, or human being, to allow you to think you are anything but a man or woman in anyone's eyes!! You are a human being, and as such, you are on the same level as they are, and nothing they say, or do, will ever change that! NOTHING!! So, why go out like that? Put a face to your name and number, show the world who you are, and let them see the things that you have accomplished, since that day you received that death sentence. Let them see the life you have made, and the friendships you have cultivated, the family that loves you, and let the world know that this is a human being that will not be silenced, until that final gasp from the poison that runs in your veins!! Stand up and fight for the next man that follows after you, give that man or woman the courage to see that track that you laid for him or her, so that they can do the same for the next human being that comes after.

Brothers and sisters, so long as we continue to allow the state to MURDER us without a peep from us . . . we will remain faceless and nameless inmates with just a number, lost and forgotten, and the senseless MURDERS will go on unabated, and we will never see the end of this madness. We are the only ones that can truly give the Abolishment Movement the momentum and voice to be heard. Through our fight for humanity and sacrifice, we will bring this struggle to forefront of the minds of the citizens across the United States! We can do this my brothers and sisters, with the courage and fortitude that I know we possess. We can do this, all we have to do is FIGHT!! AGAIN, WHAT WILL YOU DO??!!

I have spent many hours in the dayrooms, speaking to many who "claim" that they are down for the revolution. Well, to them I say this: This is Revolution that IS. This is REAL revolution. Because in this fight, it's not about winning or losing on a personal level, there are no ego meters on the door. It's about playing the game by OUR rules! Forcing the state to recognize that this is no longer a simple matter, and by your actions you give weight to the very organizations that are *now* able to move forward, rather than remain in the stagnated state that they have been in for the last few years. The movement for abolishment has stalled, and I believe that is because it has no soul, nothing to work with, no backbone to fall on, toothless, gumming food and speeches like some sick animal, lost and confused, without a purpose, feeding on *itself* rather than the enemy, allowing strife to divide, rather than unite. But, say we give that movement some teeth? Some fortitude? Showing, by example, that they are now joined by the committed from WITHIN?!!

But, in order for it to work, it must come from us. WE must be the living revolution, we must be that revolution within!! We must be willing to sacrifice one thing, because it's really the only thing you will lose, and that's your last meal! Your life is over, that is not in doubt, your visit will be over because you will not begin your fight with the state after they have gone . . . so what's left? Your meal and that's it. They have nothing else to offer you except a reprieve, and I wouldn't hold my breath for that!! Give up the meal and you go out like you're supposed to, and make your statement to the world and allow the people that love you and support you to take courage from you, and let them see that you're fighting, let the rest of the state see that you are a HUMAN BEING and there is a MURDER about to be committed in the state of Texas!! Kick and scream and fight, and take away that comfort zone that self-righteousness attitude, kick it away and show them to be what they are . . . a bunch of criminals who have taken what only God has the right to take . . . YOUR LIFE!! Let them feel *that*, when they go home that night, let that be the seed that gets planted in their sub-consciousness, let that twist in their minds and fill their dreams at night, because you have nothing to lose, NOTHING!! They are about to take the only thing worth having, and that's LIFE!!

We have the power to help change the way the people of this state, and all over the United States, think about the death penalty!! You won't win the fight, my brothers and sisters, and there won't be anyone about to help you, not at that moment, for you are alone, just you and the men and women that want to help kill you, but . . . it's not about winning, and it's not about losing, it's about forcing the world to drop what they are doing and see YOU, and only YOU, as a HUMAN BEING, you as the man you are, as the woman that you are, the persons that you became, it's about putting a human face to the death penalty, someone that they can see and identify, not just the name and number that they are used to. It's about being more than a passing mention in the local news outlets. Let the world ring and echo with the screams of a human being, who is making his or her last stand against the injustice that they are being forced to face! Let the media carry THAT story in the papers and on TVs across the United States and to the world, and believe me brothers and sisters, then we have their attention, then we have the eyes of the world on us, and with that simple act of defiance, we have brought it to the forefront, where it belonged in the first place!

Not buried in the back of some local paper, but front and center, to be read about with their coffee and rolls in the morning, and as they sit and read, they feel their breakfast begin to turn in their stomachs, the sweat begins to pour on their foreheads, and the sudden urge to pray begins to take them. As the gaze of the Almighty God is on them, and then . . . then . . . we have their attention.

And, it all begins WITHIN, from within, we will attempt to force the rules of the game that the state plays, to be changed, and it all hinges on the struggle of the inmate. He or she must be willing to do what she or he would normally do when someone is trying to kill them. That is simple.

I ask that each and everyone of you look deep within your own souls, and see if you have the courage to do what you have done all your life . . . FIGHT! And, if you do, then you can do this. And, while you're fighting for your life, the people that believe that the justice that the state is about to give you is morally wrong, and against the beliefs that they hold true, will be fighting their own fight, protesting your treatment, and showing the state and the world its disgust with a system that doesn't value human life. And, they will take heart knowing that while they are outside, letting the world know that a HUMAN BEING is being MURDERED, you are inside, fighting, and making that machine cough and choke on the gallows bait that it thinks will be easy meat!!

Let the media that has chairs in that room see a HUMAN BEING, fighting and protesting, with each grunt, scream, yell, the murder that's taking place. Let them write about that!! LET THE REVOLUTION START FROM WITHIN!!

"Better to have fought in vain, than to not have fought at all."

In the struggle,
Anibal "Bigfoot" Canales, Jr.

Ivan Cantu
#999399

Age: *35*
Hometown: *Plano, Texas*
Last school: *Plano Senior High School*
Education: *Twelfth grade*
Interests: *Freedom, politics, education, health care, traveling*
Favorites: *Movie - A Walk in the Clouds; Authors - Truman Capote and Norman Mailer*

Pressing Through a World Where I Merely Exist

Surviving Texas Death Row isn't just about sitting here on a daily basis. It's much more than that and it requires one to stay sane. Anyone that states this place doesn't bother them isn't telling the truth. Each and every day is a mental struggle. To the outside world our problems would seem menial, but in here something as simple as not getting clean sheets could cause one to commit suicide. I've never been pushed to this limit, but I have seen it occur. Each and every morning I wake with worry and concern. It's not easy but things can be done to minimize these feelings. How could I not worry when my surrounding environment always reminds me of death? Plus it never gets easy seeing the ones you know led to death. We don't actually see them being led to the gurney, but if you're housed on a pod which includes death watch, you clearly see them being led to the Walls Unit where the execution takes place.

When asked by a dear friend to write for this I was a little confused. A day in the life on Death Row is different for each of us. Plus all of our days start at different times. Sure, a schedule is offered for the officers to follow, but really our days just blend together. As Norman Mailer once said, "If we push through what we dread, the act in itself will keep us from thinking about the dread we face." To me there is a lot of truth to the statement. On Texas Death Row we don't live; we merely exist. Each day I push through fighting noise pollution, undercooked food, dirty necessities, and guards that see us as nothing. Not all guards are this way, but most of them are. Unlike other inmates we aren't given the opportunity to work. Everything we do relies on the help of others. Prior to prison I never knew inmates must purchase their own shampoo, deodorant, toothpaste and additional food items so we wouldn't go hungry.

Around here nothing is worse than being hungry. The meals served are always undercooked and never enough. I'm not a very big person, but I feel sorry for the really big guys because if the meal trays aren't going to fill me, I know they are definitely still hungry.

Day after day I live in a world where I rely on the outside for help and I don't have control of the simplest things. The outside world would probably say "good, that is what those guys deserve," but in here it's much more than that. Especially for the ones who have very strong claims of INNOCENCE. I agree with keeping criminals off the street, but I don't agree with implementing mind games and mental torture.

Unlike other inmates we aren't allowed to view television, so we have no idea how the outside world is changing. Our window to the world is through pictures in magazines, newspapers or pictures our friends send in. We're held from group recreation and any human contact at all. Of course we're held by a guard while being escorted, but we're deprived of the normal things prison society has to offer. General population inmates are allowed to have contact visits with family, but not us. You would think since Death Row inmates are sentenced to death they would be able to touch their loved ones. Not on Death Row because the concept doesn't exist. Try living in a world where you lock yourself in the bathroom for years. In a sense this is how we live. Although we don't have a shower in our cell, so that is where the difference lies.

Speaking of showers, try living in a world where you can never control the water temperature. Something so simple doesn't seem so bad to the outside world, but in here it can break a person. We have to shower and there's nothing worse than hitting the "shower button" and getting nothing but ice cold water. It never fails. It's either ice cold in the winter months or scalding hot in the summer months. On occasion the water is lukewarm but it's rare. Some days the water is so hot you can't even stand underneath it because you'll get burned. The unit can simply turn the boiler down, but they don't because if the showers are extremely hot, most inmates won't shower, which lowers the workload of the officers, and this is mainly what they care about.

Around here recreation only consists of placing us in a larger cage. A pull-up bar is provided, but really the only thing to do is walk in circles—unless of course it's our outside day—but then again we're only placed in an outdoor cage. It includes a basketball goal but it doesn't take long for this to get old. Even when outside, we're only able to see the sky. The outside recreation yard consists of three cement walls and a glass one so inside the officers can see what we're doing. Two inmates are allowed outside, but we're still divided by steel bars, so that is as close to group recreation as we'll get.

I have to say, one thing I miss is the sun. We never get even sunlight, and depending on when we're placed outside, we might never get any. Each day the recreation times fall on different hours of the day. Some days I might be outside when the sun is overhead, and on others I might not ever see it. Keep in mind we're only allowed outside two days a week, so many variables come into play when trying to absorb a little sunlight. For me one of the hardest things to deal with is all the banging and clanging of steel. Everything is steel and cement, so everything is very loud and it echoes through here. When the doors open and close, it's so loud. We're fed through a bean-slot on our cell door, and even the sound of it will make you cringe. In time I thought I would get used to it but it's only gotten worse. See, to you I'm sure these seem like minimal problems, but for the ones who live in a cage all day these simple things can make someone crazy.

And it's sad to see it happen to people around here. Once a day an inmate will seem fine but slowly and surely you'll see him change. Some are more difficult to spot than others, but anyone who is sane can witness the transformation. One inmate in particular stood in the dayroom and rubbed feces all over his body thinking it was lotion. Most inmates hollered for him to stop, but others encouraged it because they viewed it as entertainment. When in reality the inmate in the dayroom was so lost and confused that in his mind he thought he was covering his body with lotion, not even realizing it was himself that previously used the restroom in the dayroom.

One thing I noticed about this place is that time ticks different for each person. The ones closer to an execution date say that time is moving way too fast, and due to their circumstances I can see why. As for me, the time moves very slow. It seems like each day takes a week. A week takes a month and so on. I think you get the picture, but I'm sure the closer I get to the end of my appeals, the clock will tick faster.

What's crazy is on the flip side to this, when visiting someone the time flies. Two hours at visitation can seem like twenty minutes. But back here in these cells, twenty minutes can seem like two hours.

Dealing with worry and concern each and every day can take its toll, especially when we're left in the dark by our court-appointed attorneys. Nothing is worse than sharing valuable information with your attorney and them not having the decency to write back. Some of this information can actually remove us from death row. But since most of us are court appointed, they simply don't care. Don't get me wrong, I'm sure some good court appointed attorneys exist but not the one I had. I have a very strong claim of INNOCENCE but my previous attorney failed to investigate the facts. My case can be backed by DNA evidence, but it takes money to get these tests done. What is crazy is that the prosecution ordered testing for trace evidence to be halted in my case. It wasn't until I was already convicted and sitting on Death Row that I realized the severity of the prosecution stopping these tests. Normally, before sending someone to Death Row, don't you think the prosecution should test all the evidence gathered from the crime scene? Exactly. But in my case they didn't. However, I'm not the only one because many of us here were railroaded. I won't cover too much about my case because it isn't the subject of this letter, but it's very frustrating to live here knowing my previous attorney truly didn't care about my life. How could one not worry knowing we're kind of left for dead? Sure our heart beats, we breathe, we can talk; but here we don't live, we merely exist.

If it wasn't for a few friends that care about me, I'm sure I'd lose my mind. But even then it's embarrassing to ask for help. But without help I wouldn't have the basic necessities. Thank GOD for decent loving people on the outside who care, otherwise I wouldn't be able to purchase additional food items from the commissary, so I don't go hungry.

This is probably corny to share, but I'm going to share it anyway. Something as simple as Coca-Cola from the commissary will brighten my day. When living in the free world I never noticed it. But when you pop the top of a Coca-Cola the smell of freedom is released. On commissary days I'm able to smell freedom just by purchasing a Coca-Cola. See, it sounds corny and silly but it's the truth. For others it might be something different but for me it's the smell of a Coca-Cola.

Of course I get through this place by reading, writing letters and listening to the radio but if it wasn't for having the most wonderful wife, I'm sure I'd be crazy by now. I hate prison but one thing it the most wonderful wife. She tries to visit each week, but because of finances it's just not possible. She is truly the most amazing woman and she does everything in her power to show me I'm loved. I wish all the other inmates could experience the love we share, but I'm not even sure if it's possible.

My wife and I met through a mutual inmate while I was helping them communicate through letters. She was a student writing a paper having to do with mental retardation and the death penalty. Since the inmate she was in contact with was retarded, they had trouble communicating and I assisted them so she could complete her paper. We continued to write as friends, but it didn't take long before we fell in love. Of course as friends she called me out on many things, and after hours of research she uncovered that I was telling the truth about my conviction. Since then she has been doing everything she can to find someone to help us. Bless her heart because she works so hard, and I'm always proud of her. I continually pray that others will come along to help us.

The majority of the hard work is over, and at this point it's about raising additional funds to help with testing some evidence items. I can definitely say she was heaven sent and I'm blessed to have her in my life. She isn't the jealous type and she thoroughly understands I need friends in my life, so please feel free to write. In fact, I encourage it because we both enjoy meeting new people. Writing never gets old because it's always good to communicate with the outside world.

When I first arrived I used to look at the crazy people as being weak, but now I realize it's the environment that molds them. Of course some of us are going to turn crazy because of the way we're housed. Seriously, picture locking yourself in the restroom for years, and only being allowed out for a couple of hours each day. On top of that throw in someone passing your food with hair on it through the hole. It doesn't happen all the time, but on several occasions the meal trays have hair on them. You know you've been here too long when it no longer grosses you out. It just becomes part of life around here. This is how we live except it's more tortuous. The law states that criminals must be removed from society, and I agree with this, but no one should have to endure the mental torture we face on a daily basis. The state is clearly breaking the law by housing us in this way, but no one has the resources or means to fight it. We just have to deal with it along with all the other mental games we're dealt on a daily basis.

From the time I wake up until the time I fall asleep . . . I'm not living . . . I'm merely pressing through a world where I just exist.

blessed me with was the most wonderful wife. She tries to visit each week, but because of finances it's just not possible. She is truly the most amazing woman and she does everything in her power to show me I'm loved. I wish all the other inmates could experience the love we share, but I'm not even sure if it's possible.

My wife and I met through a mutual inmate while I was helping them communicate through letters. She was a student writing a paper having to do with mental retardation and the death penalty. Since the inmate she was in contact with was retarded, they had trouble communicating and I assisted them so she could complete her paper. We continued to write as friends, but it didn't take long before we fell in love. Of course as friends she called me out on many things, and after hours of research she uncovered that I was telling the truth about my conviction. Since then she has been doing everything she can to find someone to help us. Bless her heart because she works so hard, and I'm always proud of her. I continually pray that others will come along to help us.

The majority of the hard work is over, and at this point it's about raising additional funds to help with testing some evidence items. I can definitely say she was heaven sent and I'm blessed to have her in my life. She isn't the jealous type and she thoroughly understands I need friends in my life, so please feel free to write. In fact, I encourage it because we both enjoy meeting new people. Writing never gets old because it's always good to communicate with the outside world.

When I first arrived I used to look at the crazy people as being weak, but now I realize it's the environment that molds them. Of course some of us are going to turn crazy because of the way we're housed. Seriously, picture locking yourself in the restroom for years, and only being allowed out for a couple of hours each day. On top of that throw in someone passing your food with hair on it through the hole. It doesn't happen all the time, but on several occasions the meal trays have hair on them. You know you've been here too long when it no longer grosses you out. It just becomes part of life around here. This is how we live except it's more tortuous. The law states that criminals must be removed from society, and I agree with this, but no one should have to endure the mental torture we face on a daily basis. The state is clearly breaking the law by housing us in this way, but no one has the resources or means to fight it. We just have to deal with it along with all the other mental games we're dealt on a daily basis.

From the time I wake up until the time I fall asleep . . . I'm not living . . . I'm merely pressing through a world where I just exist.

Kosoul Chanthakoummane
#999529

(Editor's note: He concludes his submission with *Dum Spiro Spero*, **Latin for "While I breathe, I hope.")**

Age: 28
Education: *Eighth grade*

I hope this letter finds you full of warm spirits, and hopefully not bored out of your mind. Here on death row, there is no more chance of learning, at least not offered by the state. However, the pursuit of knowledge is always alive and well, no matter the subject. People need to look past the writings, the art, and instead look to save our souls. It is not just a question of morals or dignity, but rather faith. So if it takes a bit of visuals to grab their attention, then it's a worthy try.

A little explanation on the art. The main thing is interpretation and I'm sure right away it should be self explanatory. But, who knows, even you may be left scratching your head.

Uncle Sam, Life (Page 196)

The Uncle Sam piece, as we know, is a symbol of America. It is a symbol and demand for action, such as to go out and vote. In this case, it's a symbol of using one's voice, that in a sea of other voices, it will truly still count. That's the beauty of America, every voice is unique and holds standing. I tried to maximize its effect, so send me a pat on the back through mail. Uncle Sam is not copyrighted, nor is this image. If anything, he belongs to us, American citizens.

"Emotional Canvas" - *Kosoul Chanthakoummane*
Fictional woman inspired by an abundance of ideas.
Starting top left, Japanese/English: Tengoku=Heaven,
Jigoku=Hell, Itami=Pain, Okuru=Resent, Keibetsu=Contempt,
Nikushimi=Hate, Shi=Death, Shōgai=Life, Ai=Love,
Dōjō=Compassion, Yurusu=Forgive, Naosu=Heal

Emotional Canvas (Page 52)

The drawing of the woman is my half hearted attempt at drawing my idea of lady Justice. She would be a Libra, to balance the scales. She would hold Yin as well as Yang. Light to dark, beginning to end.

I was inspired by an eye here, nose there, lips here, etc. from various magazines. Her features, for me, resemble a blank expression. Almost a canvas for emotions, fitting the words I attached to the borders. It is my own work.

No Time for Misery (Page 35)

Last, is the Texas watch. You'll notice that there are no numbers. Why no numbers, is for the simple fact that we've received no time sentence, so time is essentially meaningless. Were it not for appeals, we would all be in coffins or urns, our pick. Instead, time for us is the necessary stops at various courts. It may consume a few years, a decade, or possibly a quarter of a century, yet time is still of no meaning. Every extra second counts, from living a bit more longer to running an execution warrant past midnight, though for now, numbers are not on our scale. You'll notice the last destination, rather than Walls, I've singled out your beloved Huntsville. A city that endorses the death penalty ought to be more civilized, yet with the correctional industry, that is unlikely to happen.

We only hope that God-loving people can look at us as sons or daughters of theirs and let compassion win out. We are, simply put, someone's child. For the majority of us, we've no choice but to die alone, to be buried in a pauper's grave.

Take care and fight the fight always.

Dum Spiro Spero,
Kosoul

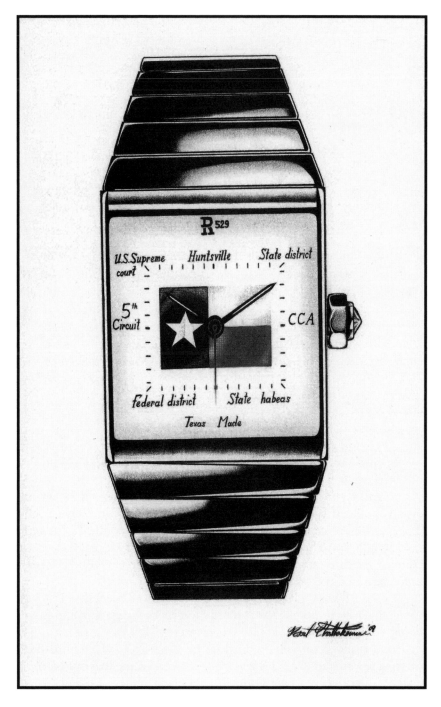

"No Time for Misery" - Kosoul Chanthakoummane

Troy Clark
#999351

Age:	*41*
Hometown:	*Never lived anywhere very long*
Last school:	*Don't remember the name of it, Granbury, Texas*
Education:	*Seventh grade*
Interests:	*Art, motorcycles, reading books, being happy*
Favorites:	*Car - 1967 Mustang Fastback; State - Oregon; Music groups - AC/DC and Metallica; Hero - Brother (RIP Bro); Book -* Where the Red Fern Grows; *Food - Tex-Mex; Movie -* Rambo.
Other info:	*Raised by Granny with brother, dirt poor moving from camp site to camp site, state to state . . . You could write a book just on my life . . . Smile!*

I'm on D/R for what my girlfriend did, I know everyone says they're innocent, I've done some shit in my day so I guess it all evens out. I just hate dying for her deal.

One night a few of us were talking here on the Row, asking questions like if you could change one thing in the world what would it be, etc. Then someone asked if you could be any kind of bird what kind would you choose? There were answers: hawk, eagle, and of course Free Bird (smile). I gave my answer instantly as a Red Bird and then answered the question why a Red Bird.

When I was a kid I shot a bird off the power line with a BB gun. As I ran up to it I bent down on my knees to see it chirping, it had blood on its beak. Man that bird was so pretty, I felt a sadness like never before. I reached to pick the bird up to try and save it. My brother's cat flew up, snatched it, and was gone . . . scared the hell out of me!!! But "if" I could be a bird I'd want to replace the one I killed.

Much respect,
Troy

Reinaldo Dennes
#999248

Age: 53
Education: Twelfth grade

I was born in Havana, Cuba on February 9, 1956, my parents and my older brother fled Cuba in 1960. I was four years old. We arrived at Miami and lived there for a few years. Moved to New Jersey and grew up there. Went to high school, received the promise of a track scholarship but never graduated. From an early age I knew I was going to be a jeweler like my father. Worked in New York until I was twenty-seven and came to Houston. Eventually opened my own jewelry store, had a beautiful home. My children are thirty-four, twenty-three, and twelve years old.

First time in prison, came when I was forty, been locked up for thirteen years now and many good things have happened to me. I must say these have been good years towards my spiritual advancement and I have evolved to a higher being.

I have realized that I'm a painter and a sculpterist, studied both Hebrew and Greek, mostly forgotten now but have read the Jewish Torah and the Greek New Testament. Studied mysticism and understand life and its mysteries more than ever.

Meditate everyday, travel within consciousness and I am one with oneness (most of the time at least in meditation).

Love to read fiction novels, just finished Noah Gordon's *The Physician.* Enjoy the classics like *Count of Monte Cristo* by Dumas, and authors like Grisham, Koontz, and many others. Never read a book until I came to prison.

I am blessed but feel sorry for the education system in America, but each one must find their own way. All religions have a grain of truth, but real truth is found within where there is a Teacher waiting for the student to appear.

I enjoy creating original work for in creation there is peace, joy, and oneness with the Creator.

I am content with my achievements in life, but also believe that in other worlds I achieve different goals so I have done everything possible under the sun.

I see myself in everyone and so treat others with kindness and compassion for we each are on a different level of awareness. So I don't judge, but also I forgive others and hope that others will forgive me.

In my older years I seem to forget many things, but I was never really educated nor graduated from high school. My first love for books was experienced here in prison. Jules Verne was my first adventure, I was forever in love with novels.

Through my studies of theology both in Hebrew and Greek, which I learned here also, the awareness of my conscious existence evolved into what I presently believe. With time and thoughts about my being, I have become aware and a little enlightened, as my artworks reflect the versions of my transformation. I am definitely not the same person both physically and spiritually, where once I was ignorant of my selfishness now I'm aware of my peaceful nature of basically reaching for my Soul in a universal consciousness of oneness. One mind, one Soul, one God.

Through meditation I receive images and ideas that I can spend a lifetime painting. This is one of the reasons I desire to live that I may communicate to the world my experience of this life. In this life, I believe I have reached a greater awareness of who I am. So I hope that next time I come I will give knowledge and beauty to these words and help those who are still imprisoned in the darkness of their ignorance.

An explanation for my artwork follows:

Universal Mind (Page 204)

Looking outside of your mind for Christ for enlightenment comes from deep within. To receive Christ and his coming is to find and know your Soul, to be one with your true essence. Your Soul will be anointed with the universal mind which can perceive and know all things of this world and the next. Let the light of peace and love shine forth.

Words Create Life (Page 203)

When two come together, the search for the Soul (Godself) one will begin to see, for two have enlightened themselves becoming one. Like two hands joined for the next great adventure, one trusting in the support of the stronger. This unification creates motion in pure consciousness, harmony with the Soul. Love, the fruit of the passion like the dove who rises to meet the mate and the two shall be one and whole again.

Ignorance Imprisons (Page 202)

When the mind is renewed—enlightened—then reason and logic are truth. The walls of bondage will crumble and the iron of oppression will melt away. The flower of beauty will blossom as love, the most precious gift when cultivated will create paradise within. From the finite to infinite and darkness-light. Where the sustenance of ignorance once thrived and enslaved, now the taste of peace and love has set me free.

The Tree (Page 205)

A good friend gave me an application for an art contest I entered, for the topic was courage. Through meditation this idea was finished in three days. The seed is your inner spirit (awareness), the earth is what imprisons or challenges the seed from becoming a tree, the tree is the maturity or the awareness, the leaves-the fruit. So the struggle to reach your inner awareness and become a tree takes courage.

Cup of Grace (Page 206)

Given to all, but who will drink from it? The drink gives life to body, mind, and spirit.

Untitled 1 (Page 207)

Stars mean, in all my paintings, a new way of thinking, a new

Christ-like consciousness. The Japanese characters mean "flow" as one with the universe. Green means in the spirit, out of the body. Male and female inside the sphere means harmony.

Untitled 2 (Page 208

This is what I think about, what's in my mind. Oneness enlightens the mind and reveals the universe.

What I have learned from my experience is that my joy and reward comes from the time of meditation through the completion of the painting. After that what happens is out of my hands and does not benefit me anyway. My desire was to reach others with this message, but no one can enlighten another unless that person first reaches in his heart and mind. I can only plant a seed; whether it grows or not is not in my power. Still, there are some here who I have inspired to paint and have reached inside for their real Teacher, and will testify as to my intentions in wanting to reveal my artwork to the world.

Peace, Reinaldo

Cesar Fierro
#000650

(Editor's note: Fierro's submission included a finger painting from some unknown brown substance that closely resembled dried blood, along with several other pieces of paper stained with the same substance.)

Age: 52
Education: Not listed

As you can see I cannot send real art by the blood or pencil or English. I know is poor and I do as best I can. Not an educated person really, just a dare of me. I do know who I am.

Free world visit and explained all I am here. See it and it's a legit. As I can. No problem. I understand all. Good luck, I take the offer as told. I am here if any problem exist.

Cleve Foster
#999470

Age: *45*
Hometown: *Henderson, Kentucky*
Last school: Midland College, Midland, Texas
Education: Fourteen years
Interests: *All outdoor activities: camping, fishing, etc.*
Favorites: *Movie* - Clan of the Cave Bear*; Car -'72 Cutlass;*
Ice cream - orange sherbet and any banana flavored dish. I also
like The Walton's *TV series. Loved them in the '70s.*
Other info: Growing up in a divorced family, I had two heroes: the
first being my mother and second, the people of my
church, "The Salvation Army."

20 Oct 08. Day 2405. 23:00

At the moment we are on lockdown due to some moron calling
a state representative on his cell phone. Leave it to some bone head
to make a move like that.

Listened to the news tonight and everyone is focusing on Death
Row, but little do they know all this started in general population.
Guards selling cell phones for $400 to $700 to the inmates in
population and then the news traveled back to death row and that
caused a few more hands to be put on the cell phones thus causing
the price to skyrocket. $2,600 to $3,000. (NO JOKE!) Now as for
people saying that people on death row are calling gang members?
Well, I can't say that doesn't happen but I can assure you, most calls
are made to loved ones and family but I'm sure that would not be
"NEWS WORTHY."

I'll also say that I don't blame people for doing what they can
to contact their loved ones.

"Untitled" - Cleve Foster

Here on death row we are allowed a five-minute call every ninety days upon request. However! I tried for three years to get a phone call and it never happened "So!" I don't blame people for taking chances with a cell phone. You?

P.S. They call me "Sarge" so feel free to do the same.

Like many people, a mother is one who has a love with endless bounds so in that respect I'm like many others, but the hero part came to life once my parents divorced. My mother did it all. She put the food on the table, tucked us in and sent us to school and saw to it that all basic needs were met but one morning sticks out in my mind that I feel moved my mother from being my mother to also my hero.

I got up early one morning during the winter, cold as heck outside so I decided to hoover over to the vent while the heat was on hoping school would be called off HAHA (Not!) Well, my mom came into the kitchen, which was next to my bedroom, sat down and was still really stiff from a full day's work the day before. Well, she sat down and was putting her socks on and I overheard her tell a family friend that she couldn't reach her feet to put her socks on and for one split moment I heard her start to cry (divorce sucks!) but that moment was short lived. Our friend asked my mom, why don't you just call in sick? You are working yourself to death! I peeked around the corner as my mom looked up and said, "I can't! I've gotta feed my babies," then she reached down, grabbed her foot, and put her socks on. Twenty minutes later, she came to each of us kids, kissed us goodbye, and went to work. "SHE NEVER GAVE UP" and is still there today.

Second. "The Salvation Army," Captain [name withheld]. Ex Army Paratrooper. The big Red One otherwise known as Ft. Campbell's best 101st Airborne. YEAH! An ex-paratrooper turned preacher and joined the Salvation Army (God's Army).

Didn't get to see my dad much after the divorce so Captain [name withheld] and a few other men of the corps filled in and told us as long as we never gave up they would be there for us and as a young man, I needed it! So with all my heart I thank them for leading by example and showing young men and women there were people who cared and knew what we were going through. (Thank God!)

Like few others I'm fighting my conviction all the way. I did NOT do this crime and after serving almost twenty-one years in the army I'm now fighting to save my own life.

The Law of Parties must be looked into further because if it's not, there's no doubt more innocent people will fall into the same situation I've fallen into. So please America!! Know your laws.

One more thing. DNA. Yup! Technology of today can serve the public in many ways and now thanks to DNA, there are people being set free from wrongful convictions thanks to the study of DNA. However! Keep in mind although DNA can help find criminals let's not forget that DNA does not mean a person committed a crime neither. So again people I say, know the laws for which you live by because if you don't ANYTHING YOU SAY WILL BE USED AGAINST YOU IN A COURT OF LAW.

People have asked me many times, does anything funny ever happen on death row and the first thing that comes to mind is, My Spider Story, OH YES! Living in a world that measures six-by-nine one tends to embellish when writing one's pen-pals, HAHA. HEY! It's boring here and nothing ever happens so cut me some slack okay. HAHA. It happened like this.

My Spider Story

I was sitting on my bunk one night writing to a pen-pal and about to wrap up yet another short and very boring letter when out of the corner of my eye I saw something move so, I looked up and saw this huge, huge, black hairy spider. The first thing I thought was, how in the world did something that big get into this prison and then I asked, why the HELL did you just come into my cell? Well, I told myself, Ahhh just toss something at it and it'll go back under the door and pester someone else. Easy enough! I reached up and grabbed a postcard and tossed it at the spider and went back to writing. Well, a couple minutes later I saw the card flying back across the floor so I looked up and this eight-legged intruder seemed to be giving me some sort of John Wayne stand off.

So, I picked up something bigger and tossed at it and would ya believe, he jumped over it. Well, needless to say I was not gonna let this ugly Arachnid front me like that so I started to take off my shoe and unload a can off whoop-ass when he made a move and started to jump. Well little did he know I was ready for him. He jumped and when he did I did my ninja turtle matrix move and as I came up I took my shoe and did my best Venus Williams back hand slapshot and sent the little sucker flying into the toilet. Then alls it took was a little wall walking and back flip and my hand was on the flush button. HAHA. OH Yeah! Down he went Hee Hee but I could swear just before he went under I heard "Heeeelp Meee." I had a dream that night and the dream ended with this HUGE spider's leg coming out of my toilet. HAHA.

GHOST! Did someone say GHOST? Yup! I'm not one to put any value on folklore unless I can say first hand that, YES! This has happened to me. Well my friend, after hearing all the tales of sightings and things moving and so on, I was sure that half the people on Texas death row were losing their minds. Well, that is until I caught something out of the corner of my eye. Hmmm did someone just walk up to my door? I'm sure I saw something so I walked to my door, looked both ways and NOTHING! This has happened many times to me so I asked others, have you ever seemed to think you've seen someone walk past your door? Huh. "ALL" told me, yes! Ooooohhh.

I've heard the cart rolling down the hallway in front of the doors downstairs so I'd yell down and ask the inmates on one row what's going on down there. HUH NOTHING! Doo-Doo-Doo-Doo. I just sat down. MAKES YA THINK HUH?

Thinking Out Loud

Just like every execution day, they all show up. The prosecution, the attorneys, media, and prison big wigs and with only one thing on their mind. "Taking a life." Putting another threat to society on the gurney. Killing in the name of justice, feeding the Texas Killing Machine.

I'm sure some of the things that [name withheld] heard were the "attaboys" as attorneys slapped themselves on one another's backs. As they think, "got another one," and the footsteps down the eighty-yard walk to the van that will take him to the Walls Unit in Huntsville where he'll die tonight. Just after 18:00 hours and then last but not least, all the TAT-TAT-TATs on the windows of all the other inmates who are watching him leave.

However! The one thing he doesn't hear are the cries of the people out at the front gate as they watch him walk down the sidewalk. They. The victims "To Be!" of yet another killing.

I hate this place! I also hate that "anyone" has to suffer the loss of a loved one. Yes! I'm sure that if it were me who had been the loved one of a person murdered. I too would seek vengeance and would want that person to rot in hell but then that would be just as bad as patting someone else on the back and saying "got another one," don't ya think?

I'm sure if Texas stays on track it will in fact take the record this year, something they strive for each year but for the most of it comes up juuust short every time, but this year it doesn't look good for the men in the white jumpers.

Well, it's recreation time and I'm going outside so I'll write more later.

15:44. Just got back from recreation and one thing I noticed when I got back in was, while at recreation, I'd forgotten all about the upcoming execution. Me and another inmate swapping stories. BS-ing about this, that, or the other.

Not one single thought of an execution . . . just another day on Texas Death Row.

Gotta go. Shower time.

Sincerely,
Sarge

PS—Texas' Death Row sucks!

Juan Garcia
#999360

Age: 28
Hometown: Houston
Last school: *Walltrip, Houston, Texas*
Education: *Seven and a half*
Favorites: *Movies* - The Power of the Dog, The Godfather; *Ice cream - strawberry; Cars - '62-'64 Impalas*

Well, to start off my life here on death row has really been hard because I was really never used to being away from my loved ones. If I was not with them I was talking with them on the phone until I would fall asleep. So it's even not all that easy me being a father of two which I have seen grow up on me since I have been locked up. It hurts because I told myself that it wouldn't happen to me and my family what happened when I was growing up and seeing my stepfather in and out of jail and prison but it is different in all of my tios and tias and stepfather and brother. I am the only one that ended up on death row.

At a young age, the age of eighteen, I was facing death right in its face being that a lot of kids just can't wait to try to do what they want to stay out as late as they want. Not me, I was trying to keep food in my son's stomach and wife's as well to keep them both healthy and because my wife was pregnant with my daughter at the time so it's really not all that easy to say that I am making it in here because the true words are that each day that I have been away from my kids I am dying a little. But with the good Lord's help I will make it out there to finally get to hold my baby girl, my daughter, in ten years who is now going to be eleven years. I still have not gotten to hold my baby girl but with a lot of praying and faith with the Lord's help I will one day finally get to hold her and tell her that I am sorry for all the years that I have missed out in her life.

Well how I spend my day. Well, working, art, reading, writing and drawing and keeping to myself as much as I can and from time to time trying to learn the reason why God lets things happen the way he does to good people. Not that I am all that good. No I may have made a real foolish mistake in being in the wrong places at the right time but only the Lord knows why he does what he does.

Well about the crime that I have been convicted of, I really don't like to talk about it because it brings back so much pain to have seen the little faces of the victim's kids, looking at the mom who is being put out of the world of the killer that killed their father and messed up their lives and family. I did write their mother and asked her to forgive me and to please believe me that it didn't happen the way they say it did but still here I sit waiting to die. A death number is all I am now to the people who don't even know the real me, the nice and sweet person that I am, but it's life if I am this cold blooded killer that just needs to be put to death.

Well special memories that I can remember are being with my wife since we got married at the age of fifteen. Yes we were still young but taking that I had gotten her pregnant and it was the right thing to do. I asked her to marry me, which we did get married in May 21, 1997 and every day since then I was always trying to make it better than the last. Then came along my son that night after being kicked and hated from my wife for putting her through so much pain from having my son, I was happy. I didn't want no one to hold my son not even my wife. It was a work of art to see that I, the fuck up that I had been in life, that I still had the life of being a father still somewhere in me and to be able to hold him and kiss him each night before I was going to bed was always the best times of my life. Even his very first word "Dada" was the best. I never did let my wife forget it which what father wouldn't. But it was fun me and my wife were still kids and still didn't know much about raising a family but with the love between the both of us we made it and never ever gave up even after all her family did to try to get us broken up we still made it—until this foolish mistake came to play a role in our lives which changed it for the both of us.

Political issues, well I have to say that I have never ever been able to forgive my mother for always picking my stepfather over me since I always had places that I could go and stay which was always a girlfriend or ex-girlfriend's place. But it's just that a little part of me died when this Mama's Boy was kicked out on the streets by his mama.

Well for who will ever take the time to read words from a person that the world sees as a cold blooded killer, I just want to say that it's not always what the book looks like on the outside. It's what's on the inside, and you will never know really know what's on the inside until you give it a chance and open it and read it. But don't just read it like if you're living it. Like if you are me and I am you is really where the book and the words in it will really start to come to life right before your eye. And never believe what you hear until you know the real story of what all has happened. Or until you get to meet that person and really get to see what he is like on the inside and not who the world has made him out to look like to the rest of the world that does not know him. So as you sit wherever you are, think how much the world has really changed and how little mistakes would have gotten looked into so good back then when someone's life was on the line then now how it always seems to get over looked or just never really have the time to find out the real story of how and what really did happen on that day.

So if I am killed by the state before you ever get to meet me all I can say that the words "An eye for an eye and a tooth for a tooth" is really not how it seems. It's just an easy way for the ones that know that they really don't have anything on you to make the rest of the world think and believe that you did do what they say you did. But now at age twenty-eight I have seen a lot of guys die and a lot cry but never have I seen one honest enough to say he was wrong but as every man lives his life the way he thinks he should or how he thinks it looks in the eyes of the ones he is trying to look good for.

So just take the time to stop and smell the roses in life because not all of them will make you sneeze. Some will put a smile up on your face when you really need one and even give you a hug when no one else will or can. So these are a few words from a so-called cold-blooded killer. Keep your eyes open and never get caught sleeping because it's always the best time that they try to get you where you really can't think all that straight. So wake up because the world does not wait for no one not even the ones that sleep walk. It's always a give and take in the world today. So I send these two drawings to show a little of a life that it has which they say that a picture is like a thousand words. So it's really not much but it's just how I feel still holding onto what little love, hope, and faith I still have and would like to share with that one special person who will just only give me the chance and time to. So take care and sweet dreams and don't let the time run out. Bet it, because life is way much more beautiful then facing death right at its face. So wake up and listen to the Lord's call.

"Untitled" - Juan Garcia

Gabriel Gonzales
#521992

Editor's note: The prisoner number above for Gonzales is for the Bexar County Jail, not Death Row, as he explains below. His number on Death Row was #999225.

Age: *35*
Education: Eighth grade

Recently I was transferred back to San Antonio for a resentencing hearing and will be here until next year until court proceedings are finalized. I may not be on Death Row next year (depending on what happens in court).

May those who read this book realize the humanity in those condemned (both guilty and innocent) to death for crimes. And may it bring understanding to all who read it.

Good and Evil—and Beyond

Go(o)d and (D)evil depend on each other like concave and convex. The same instinct in us that personifies good into God transforms evil into Devil. We put human faces on good and evil to try to humanize the universe. God created man in his image and man returned the favor. One of the reasons we create gods and angels is because we want to believe that the world is ruled by benevolent powers. But when these powers do not eliminate suffering, tragedy, and death, we evoke a panoply of devils, "walk-ins," and monsters to absorb the blame for evil.

Because gods and goddesses do not die they reassure us that something abides; beyond our time and space there is a reality invulnerable to death; the Rock of Ages is not washed away by the river. The logic of religion is reflected in the primitive practice of driving an axis mundi—a world-pole—into the ground at the place where a mystic, shaman, or priest has received a vision or revelation of God. The tribe then organizes its life around this point—the sacred center of the world. All lines radiate from the Church Steeple (or the capitol building); the holy is the centering point for human life, the firm foundation, the Eternal Rock. Paul Tillich translated this religious act into psychological language when he said that whatever concerns us ultimately is our god. Even if "God is dead" the presence of the holy permeates the place where our needs for security and meaning are met. Whatever passion is at the center of our lives—work, money, family, music, education, politics, romance—promises salvation and demands ultimate loyalty.

The Devil is still with us. The forces of evil are organized and, consciously or unconsciously, they conspire against us. They are out to get us: the terrorists, computer viruses, greedy bankers, the Pentagon, drug cartels, Big Brother, cancer, AIDS. Or (for psychological sophisticates who don't believe in projection or the Devil) evil is reduced to abstract qualities within the self: fear, hostility, passivity, repression, primal pain, or weak will.

Regardless of what we call them, our modern dualisms divide us as much as the old ones did: whether we project Good and Evil outward on God and the Devil or inward on Eros and Aggression the split remains. And a split world means a perpetual battleground between the black and white, two habitats for schizophrenics. The effort to root out the evil we create by our definitions spreads the disease. In the long run our best solution is to proclaim an armistice, an end to dualism, and welcome the warring factions in the human commonwealth. The opposites belong together, the contradictions can be encompassed. The Devil is Lucifer, God's fallen angel; Eros waits under Aggression; strength is hidden just below the fault in personality. An old Eastern Proverb sums it up: "where you stumble and fall there you will find the gold." Nietzsche pointed the way toward the unity of personality when he challenged us to go "beyond good and evil." We can trust life to break through our brittle moral judgments and rise up like a seedling from the husks of old confines.

Randy Halprin
#999453

Editor's note: Halprin is one of the "Texas Seven" mentioned in the introduction on Page 9.

Age: 31
Hometown: Arlington, Texas
Last school: Oneida Baptist Institute, Oneida, Kentucky
Education: Twelfth grade
Favorites: Book - One *by Richard Bach; Movie -* The Last of the Mohicans; *Ice cream - mint chocolate chip; Band -* The Cure
Other info: *I was adopted at age five. I'm Jewish but believe strongly in spiritualism. I believe everyone is capable of redemption and compassion. I became a vegetarian at age twenty-eight.*

If I Could Time Travel

I'm probably not the only person on earth who has wished that they had a way to travel back in time. I've been on death row now since the summer of 2003 and I often find myself staring at the empty white walls in my cell and wondering how in the world I ended up in this place. I mean, I've obviously made some very awful decisions, but is there one point in my life that I could go back to, walk up to myself and scream, "You have no idea how crazy your life is about to get if you go through with this idiot!"

It was May of 1995. I was just returning from Oneida, Kentucky having just completed my junior year. I would only be home on the summer break for three weeks and then I would return back to Kentucky to finish up an extra credit class so that there would be no doubt that I would graduate with the class of '96. I had failed my seventh grade year in Arlington, Texas and so my parents had sent me away to private school to get me back on track.

My break started out fine. I really had no more friends in my hometown, as I'd been away for a couple of years and my current friends were all in Ohio or Kentucky. So, I spent most of the time swimming and watching TV, playing with my little brothers or being on the phone with my girlfriend talking into the wee hours of morning. Other days I would sneak off to the side of our house and siphon Freon from one of the big air conditioning units and huff it until I passed out.

One day my brother and I had decided to go hang out at the mall that was about a mile away from our house. I asked my dad if we could go and if yes, could he drop us off. He said no, but we decided to go anyway by taking our bicycles.

My brother still had his bike, but I remembered that mine had been stolen not long before. Undeterred, I decided that it wouldn't be a big deal to dust off my dad's old Schwinn bicycle that he hadn't ridden in ages and use that. I cleaned the dust off and aired up the tires and off we went.

Things between my father and me were already pretty tense. Coming back from school, I was already starting to experiment with drugs, I was seriously confused about religion and who I was, but more afraid to express to my Jewish father that I was seriously considering becoming a christian. Top that off with a teenager who thought he was madly in love and you have a kid with a lot of junk gathering up in his head.

After spending the day at the mall, me and my brother rode back home. The sun was setting and I remember thinking aloud, "I wonder what dad will say since we went out anyway." And like typical teens we both thought, oh they'll get over it.

We pulled into the driveway, punched in the garage door code and took our bikes inside. I was a little nervous as we walked into the house, but to our surprise mom and dad had little to say when we went to the living room.

We told dad that we had gone to the mall and he said, "At least you boys got home at a reasonable time." And then as an afterthought,

"How did y'all get there?"

"We took our bikes," my brother said.

"Uh, I used your bike, dad because mine was stolen," I said.

"Who did you ask to ride it?" Dad said, his face beginning to redden.

"Nobody. I just figured, uh, you never use it so what's the big deal?"

"You didn't ask me."

"Didn't ask you?" I said in disbelief. "It's been collecting dust since the '70s!"

My dad looked at my mother and she shrugged as if to say "I'm staying out of this one."

"It doesn't matter if I ride it or not. It's my bike, it belongs to me. You know that you need to ask whenever you're going to use something that's not yours," my father said.

"Yeah, okay dad, like I'm going to ask to use it when you said we couldn't go in the first place," I fired back.

I knew I was in the wrong but I refused to back down because I felt like he was just picking a fight. "Well, you're grounded now. No using the car, no going out until I decide that you can and until I get an apology."

"What? I didn't even do anything!"

"This conversation is over, Randy. Go to your room."

"Man, this is my summer break. I'll do whatever I want to do!" I yelled, stomping off.

Later that night I called my girlfriend. "Hey?" I asked as she got on the phone. "Hey, honey! I thought you'd never call back."

"You are not going to believe the crap that's going on. I'm grounded!" I said.

"For what? Oh, did your parents tell you that I called earlier?" she asked.

"They never told me you called. Huh. Anyway, I rode my dad's bicycle to the mall with my brother and he about blew a gasket. He's never ridden the damn thing." The conversation carried on until early the next morning.

The next day my dad and I continued to fight. He told me that part of my punishment would be to help him build tables in the garage with no pay. I felt like the little bit of summer I had was gone.

Being the impulsive person that I can be at times, an idea began to brew in my mind. I loved my dad to pieces, but I was so mad that I was letting this fight get the best of me. I needed to get away from the house. It seemed like they didn't really want me around anyway, and so I called my girlfriend up and told her my plan. I'm not sure if she took me seriously, but she didn't try to talk me out of it, so I took it as a green light. I asked if she'd call one of our friends in Louisville, Kentucky who lived in her area and see if I could stay at his place. She asked me how I'd pay for the ride to get back to Kentucky but I lied, telling her that I already had enough money to cover it.

I hung up the phone and called the Greyhound bus station and asked how much it would cost for a one way ticket to Louisville, Kentucky.

I nearly choked when the service lady told me almost two hundred dollars. Where on earth would I come up with that kind of money?

That night I paced back and forth, I just wanted to leave. Get out now. A brief idea flashed across my mind, but I tried to chase it off. Yet, several minutes later I found myself in my dad's office and holding his business cheques in my hand. I forged a two hundred dollar cheque, went back to my room, and hid it, then fell asleep.

I did spend the next couple of days building tables for my dad. When I was finished, I'd go off and get high. I thought about calling the whole thing off, as I hadn't yet cashed the cheque and just tell dad I was sorry and try to patch things up, but I wouldn't let it go. I was so angry and confused. I felt like my girlfriend was the only person who could relate with the things I was struggling with and I'd rather be with her, be with someone who understood me.

I packed up the things I'd be taking back to Kentucky with me and wrote mom and dad a little note trying to justify what I was doing. I knew they'd be hurt and angry, but it was just something I had to go through with. When I was done with that, I went out to the garage and grabbed my brother's bike and rode off to the bank with the forged cheque in my pocket. Once I had cashed it I realized there was really no turning back now. I came back home with two hundred dollars.

Dad was out on some business errands and my brother was in our game room playing Nintendo with my two youngest brothers. I told him what I planned to do and gave him explicit instructions to not give the note I'd written to my parents until I was already gone. He asked me why I was leaving and I told him that it was just something I had to do.

I said goodbye to my two youngest brothers. They hadn't any idea of what was going on and it pained my heart that I'd be leaving them behind. Had I known that it would be the last time I ever saw them again, I wouldn't have left. I hugged them and told them I loved them.

Dad came back home at the end of the day and started getting dinner ready. He asked me if I wanted to help, as he knew that this was something I really enjoyed doing with him. "Nah, I'm alright," I replied.

I went back to my room and called a taxi cab and then my girlfriend to let her know that I was on my way. Ate dinner with my family quickly and then told them I was going outside to think. They excused me and I went out to the garage where my brother had helped me sneak my luggage out. Suddenly I missed our long gone cat, Tiger, wishing he was there at my feet, rolling around and purring for me to rub his belly. I could hear my brothers laughing inside and my brother asked, as if reading my thoughts, if this was something that I really wanted to go through with. My shoulders sagged and I reached for him to give him a hug. "I'm sorry, but this is something I've got to do. You wouldn't understand."

As we were hugging my dad came outside. I looked at him and he looked at me. "Hey," he said. "Hey." I said back. "I was thinking that you and I could talk. I'm going to pick up a few things from Krogers. Want to come along?" Then he threw me the keys to the car. It was his way of saying, "Hey, let's make up." I threw the keys back and told him I'd stay here. A sad looked crossed his face as he got into the car and drove off. A few minutes later the taxi cab pulled into the driveway. We loaded my luggage into the trunk and I gave my brother one last hug. "Don't forget to give them the note," I told him and then and got into the cab.

Mom and Dad,

I don't expect you to understand what's going on with me. I'm just going to Louisville for the rest of the break. I do have a place to stay and I will go back to school when it opens back up. I'm not running away. I just need a break. I'll call you when I get there. I promise.

Love,
Randy

I never did call when I got to Louisville and I never came home again. The following year spiraled out of control. I was using drugs regularly. I was beginning to steal and lie often. I got kicked out of school and then in September of 1996 I went to jail after I acted out in violence on LSD. In December of 2000 me and six other inmates escaped from prison, leading to a robbery and death of a police officer. I didn't participate in the shooting, but was convicted and sentenced to death by the Texas Law of Parties.

I do believe that if I had that time machine and went back to 1995 my whole life would be different. But that's stuff for the movies. All I can do now is face my mistakes and try to live out what life I have left in recognition of my faults and bad choices and try to be the best human that I can be, whatever fate may bring.

Ray Jasper
#999341

Age: 28
Hometown: San Antonio
Education: Dropout
Interests: Justice and truth
Favorites: Million Dollar Habits *by Brian Tracy and the Bible are the books that have impacted my life.*
Other info: *I firmly believe judgment in America is fleeting. People love you when you're down. We need to treat others the way we'd want to be treated if we were them.*

The New Oppression

The word oppression has gotten lost in the American vocabulary. Today, if you were to ask most Americans where people are being oppressed by the government they would point you to the far Middle East or China or some other place than America. But imagine if you were sentenced to one hundred years in prison.

In the 1980s and 1990s due to the rise in gang violence and crack cocaine in major cities across the United States, lawmakers sought out to change laws to become " tough on crime" and treat those who violate the law as examples to the rest of society. Today, over two million people are in the United States prison system. The largest prison population in the world. The courts are passing down multiple life sentences, one hundred years, even two hundred years. Literally the court system is locking people up and throwing away the key. People under the age of twenty-five with their first offense are receiving death sentences, life and life without parole.

While politicians and lawmakers judge crime from their standpoint they never consider what happens to those people who have received these sentences. Rather than seeing people, the system just sees paperwork to be filed. Chuck Colson, former advisor of the president, once wrote: "We were passing laws to be tough on crime, but we really didn't know who they were affecting." It wasn't until the Watergate scandal and Colson himself was locked up that he had a tremendous change of heart. In his book *The God of Spiders and Stones*, Colson frowned on the entire American prison system. He predicted that by the year 2000, America would have built a society within a society by investing in prisons. The book was definitely on point.

Prison is now a society of its own in America. Instead of being rehabilitated and returned to normal society, individuals are given sentences beyond their life expectancy and are forced to spend their entire lives living in prison and, most significant, dying in prison. America is the only nation in the world to sentence criminals to time beyond a normal human life span.

Do Americans believe slavery was oppression?

If the answer is yes, then under the 13th Amendment of the U.S. Constitution, Americans have to consider the prison system oppression. Under the 13th Amendment all prisoners are constituted to be slaves.

One may argue if people break the law, they deserve to be forced to pay their debt to society. Yet looking at today's leaders, we have seen many politicians take sworn oaths and break the law. Countless prosecutors have purposely mishandled cases; police officers have brutalized and even killed harmless people in the line of duty; judges have been shown corrupt; and politicians have received bribes.

The truth of the American government is it's the most hypocritical system in the world. What we see is too much makeup on the face of the government concealing its blemishes from the rest of the world, being made to look as if nothing is wrong through politically correct behavior. Nixon, Bush, Clinton, Wade, Spitzer, Rosenthal and many others have all been the subject of political scandal. Many have openly lied to the public.

Governing officials get caught in their sins, appear on TV and make a public apology, then everyone forgives and forgets. Ordinary people get caught in their sins and their apologies are useless. They are prosecuted to the fullest extent of the law. If the American people cannot recognize *oppression* and the oppressor, then we passively accept lawlessness and hypocrisy in the government arena. Public apologies and politically correct behavior does not amount to justice.

Corruption in the legal system needs to be dealt with, not swept under the rug. Corruption in the political arena by those who take sworn oaths to integrity needs to be dealt with like all criminal activity. Only then will justice by served.

Derrick Johnson
#999339

Age: 28
Hometown: *West of Dallas*
Last school: *South Oak Cliff High School, Dallas, Texas*
Education: *Tenth grade*
Interests: *Since I have a probing mind, I would say origins.*
Favorites: *I don't have a specific book, but teachers I favor are*
Alan Watts, Malcolm X, Yogananda (Indian master).
Movies - Braveheart, Scarface, Cooley High, Coming
to America, School Daze*; Ice cream - cookies and cream;*
Car - Cadillac

Life on death row is like life at its fundamental root: A paradox of contrast. In seeking the one-dimensionalism of my whole nature (while as a man free the paradox of contrast where cultivated characteristics require their own space), the battle of the man I was the day before, the new man trying to burst forth, and these two, clash. Only one fear I have discovered that I have—the fear of being the greater part of myself with the breadth of vision and clarity of thought that commands the yielding of profound truths of life, because it is not native to my familiarity. I am aware of the refinement occurring and the impurities melting away by the flames of the struggle, but I can't keep a weary eye from the rearview, which in moments of clarity often proves that I'm like the insect with the wrong fascination to the flame. To remain as I appear; to contradict what formerly was known, is the contrast. That belongs to the world's observation. The paradox is in trying to show poise of one over the other, and belongs to me. If I am to be the totality of who I am, then I will offend some, cause opposition and criticism (Jesus was the exemplar of such). The day of vindication is a moment best left to history. The paradox can only be understood by those strong enough to stand in truth, and who defy contemporary norms.

One of the most easily perceived qualities of life on death row is the many deprivations. Simple science reveals that if you isolate, restrict and suppress to one extreme, the direct opposite extreme will manifest. The exception here is being aware of the controlling center. Because of the depravities many thrust themselves up with things of no worth. The greater majority that have been here for a good number of years are prone to psychosis that they are surely unaware of. Every man must face his strengths and weaknesses and decide where he wishes to rest. As I intimated above, my life on death row is the maintenance of strength and the quality of endurance to see the life of myself based on a new knowledge that will bring new order. Since I am one who intelligently battles, I conserve my nature for those of like nature.

I spend my time pursuing what I'm led to. A deep probing of my circumstances and present experiences propels me. In a sense, it's like the moment before I compose a poem or a letter. It is a state felt; an unforced flow that produces things that leaves me speechless. I write constantly, working out my ideas on pertinent subjects of life.

One special memory that is indelibly etched on my brain is the time that my mother sought to teach me how to be a responsible man by leaving me alone with my three-month-old son in 1998. I was seventeen years of age. My mother watched as I dressed myself in casual wear preparing to go out and meet some ladies—an adventure of mine and a best friend who was more like a brother. As I was about to leave, she stopped me and explained that he was my child, and that the weekend arrangements of having him was so that we could bond and I could learn to allocate my priorities, and then she left the house. For an instance I was mad. But once we begin to roll on the floor and I changed his Pampers and warmed his bottles and put him to sleep on my chest, I felt things that I obviously within those moments did not comprehend. Because of that and other times, and maturation, it is now that I understand what my mother was doing. Those experiences were invaluable, and now are the sweetest things I'll ever know.

In closing, it is imperative to know, in the sense of commanding all situations, that the attainment of awareness should be accounted as the crowning virtue, and is lucidly self-evident. To feel one's own imperfections, and to demonstrate the strength to fight against them is the essence of humanity. Many tell the story of sleepers, whose memorials will exhaust prematurely. But as one awakened by life and sorrow, I bear a truth that will endure. So my life on death row is a struggle of equanimity, a testament of fortitude, and a story of indomitable will.

Texas Death Row Art: A Gallery

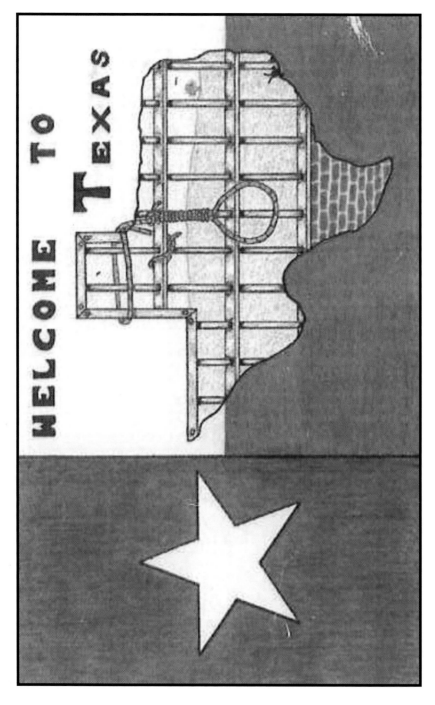

"Welcome to Texas" - Perry Austin

"Uncle Sam, Life" - Kosoul Chanthakoummane

"Ride Free" - Troy Clark

"The Rose" - Troy Clark

"Dragon" - Cleve Foster

"Poeta of Life" - *Charles Thompson*
If you dreamt of a flower in a wonderful dream,
and when you dreamt that flower was in your
hand . . . and when you awoke from your
dream—in your hand was that flower. . .what then?

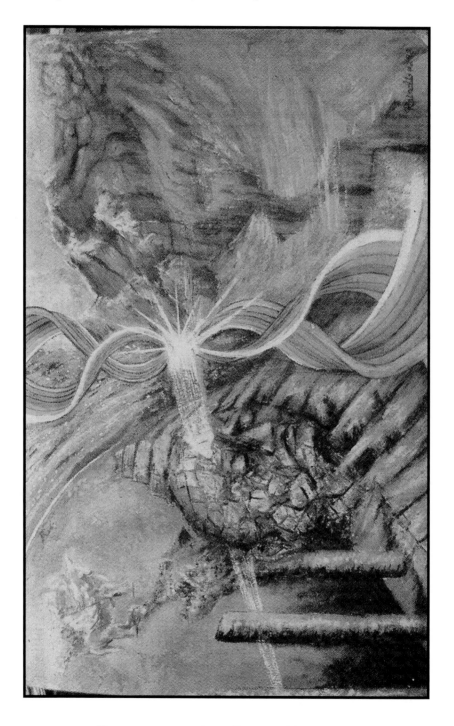

"Ignorance Imprisons" - *Reinaldo Dennes*

"Words Create Life" - Reinaldo Dennes

"Cup of Grace" - Reinaldo Dennes

"Untitled 1" - Reinaldo Dennes

"Untitled 2" - *Reinaldo Dennes*

"Universal Mind" - Reinaldo Dennes

"Native Girl" - Troy Clark

"Me" - Cleve Foster

"Fingerpainting with Unknown Substance" - Cesar Fierro

David Lewis
#000866

Age: *53*
Education: *Twelfth grade*

Window of Death

My name is David Lewis. I am an inmate on Texas Death Row and I have been here going on twenty-three years. I live in a cell on the death pod, this is where the men with execution dates live. I have a small window in my cell that I can look out of whenever I want. I look out of it every day to see what the day is like. Sometimes it is nice and sunny and sometimes it is raining and nasty. My window overlooks the parking space where they bring inmates into the unit. I watch this every day to see who is coming or going. But most of all I watch for the transfers van that comes to take the condemned man away.

I have given my window a name. It is called the "Window of Death." I have seen so many men taken away to never be seen again. As I watch the guards bring the man I am wondering what he is thinking on his last day. I often wonder what I would be thinking as I stepped into that van. Is there anyone looking out of their window of death at me wondering the same thing? My heart is heavy with sadness to see so many men taken away to be murdered to teach us not to murder.

The van comes to set another soul free today. Is he a lucky one? He doesn't have to endure this hell anymore so I guess he is lucky. Pick up a gun, swing a knife, take a life, you can have your very own window of death in just a few nights.

Please set my soul free so I don't have to see another man step into that damn van! Window of death I paint you black, now it's time I turn my back. I look my friend in the eye and say, let me take your place because now I want to die.

Charles Mamou, Jr.
#999333

Age: 34
Hometown: Sunset, Louisiana
Last school: Beau Chene High School, Grand Coteau, Louisiana
Education: Twelfth grade
Interests: Playing basketball, writing, and meeting new people
Favorites: Movies - Usual Suspects and A Time to Kill; Book - The
            Alchemist by Paulo Coelho; Car - Cadillacs
Other info: "When you are aware of who you are, it doesn't matter what
            others say you are not."

Greetings and peace always. I hope this day brings you some happiness and joy.

I received your letter seeking writers for your book/project. And immediately felt I had to be a part of it. Just to be heard if nothing else. Why you think inmates and "cash" payments are harmonious is beyond me. The majority of inmates do not always want something for their participation in a project that will become ridiculed by some. Having said such, you're seeking articles from Texas Department of Criminal Justice housed inmates but restrict us from grievancing about TDCJ's treatment.

But if I was one of them nappy-headed guys from that prison in Guatemala (or wherever) then y'all be wanting to know about the mistreatment and abuse of policy that eventually abuses inmates, right here in Texas. But I understand, TDCJ affiliate. No harm. No foul. (smile).

Enclosed you will find my article. And I will be expecting my free book.

Understand Self First

Friedrick W. Nietzsche, a German philosopher once quoted, "He who has a 'why' to live for can bear with almost any how." Viktor E. Frankl added this insight with regards to Nietzsche's quote, "This could be the guiding motto for all psychotherapeutic and psycho hygienic efforts, regarding prisoners."

When I read these two quotes by these two thinkers, I came to conclude my own view: "Whether you are a prisoner of concrete walls, iron bars and razor wire fences, or social and economic woes, or mental insecurities, we all need, hunger—in fact, thirst for a 'why' in this world to live through just one more day."

My name is Charles "Chucky" Mamou Jr., and I am a Texas Death Row prisoner since 1999. I write to you without any acrimony, although should I allow my words to be injected with anger, rage, or an unmasked disdainment, I would feel justified in allowing my words to become cacophonous in nature. However, one thing about doing time in which doing time has become banal, complaints are a sure sign of defeat, when all one does is complain without any labor to back it up. Or as Congresswoman Shirley Chisholm so eloquently noted in a 1974 speech in Kansas City: "One does not learn, nor does one assist in the struggle, by standing on the sidelines, constantly complaining and criticizing. One learns by participating in the situation—listening, observing, and then 'acting.'"

And so, I find myself a student of my own self. I come to you as a man—an imprisoned man whose mental incarceration has been pardoned. I see things now with clarity. Without bias or discernment. For nothing is without meaning. And no one goes through this life without having meaningful obligation, regardless to one's status quo.

It is my aphorism that, "Evolution has nothing to do with the creation of the physical. Rather evolution has everything to do with the intellectual molding of the mental man. What he believes or disbelieves. What he allows to be taught and corrected."

Having said all that, I contest without seeking any sympathetic petitions that I'm not the same man I was ten years ago. Now don't get it twisted, my imprisonment and death sentence did not bring about such change. My dereliction of my one ignorant mindset has brought anew within me. For any person to fully attempt to start the process of change, it has to start with the changing or reforming of one's mind. I've never been one who took a liking to the cliché, "You Are

What You Think Yourself To Be." A criminal does not walk around daily thinking about what sermon he's going to preach on Sunday. Nor does he sing Amazing Grace repeatedly. No, he's thinking about his next heist or illegal act. And so within these mental corridors, I've come to accept what many would deem the unacceptable: "Humans do change!" Some from good to bad—and yet such rules apply for the 'bad' too. Many do change from bad to good.

Life has a meaning if there is a purpose. Or as Nietzsche concluded—a 'why.' Why we laugh? Why we love? Why do we crave for the affection of the one person who we find so libidinous? These whys along with cautious hindsight allow us to decipher what is important to us. What allows us to impregnate sanity into our daily thoughts, judgments, and acts.

For me, such sanity—or 'help' comes from my devotion to my mother, children, family, and sincere friends. More importantly the devotion they have for me sustains me. Keeps me smiling when my face is scarred with caked frowns. They help levee-tize my eyes so that my tears do not cause my heart to flood into misery. They are the real reasons for my many 'whys' in which I continue to live with hope. My family has allowed me to see the other 'victims' of the Death Penalty. The victims who go unnoticed, uncounted, unheard of and unspoken about. And as much as I understand that it's my own actions that have allowed the ones I love to become victims. I see an incredible resiliency in them that is such as afflatus beckon, that ignorance . . . my own ignorance is not my mental master of chaos anymore.

I don't know what tomorrow is going to bring. And nor am I concerned about a day that hasn't yet decided to come. I can only concern myself with the now. And how my edification in the now will allow me to be a better person in the tomorrows that lay ahead—should any tomorrows come to past. And I can smile from ear to ear at this moment, because I am ALIVE. "Was mich nicht umbringt, macht mich starker" (is German for, "That which does not kill me, makes me stronger"). And indeed I am stronger and wiser in mind, if nothing else. Stronger today than I was yesteryears.

Life isn't how you see it. It's how you make it. There's a need for leaders who won't just talk about the ills of a nation and its people, rather—will lead by their own sweat, blood, and tears in a righteous, veracious dejure. No matter where you are, or how the minority of ignorant people view you. A Change Is Going to Come, if you embrace yourself to accept it. A change within you has merit when you educate others in a responsible manner.

Observation is nine-tenths of the law of mankind and of our dwellings within nature. It's what we observe that allows us to become enlightened and studious. To become aware of, and accountable to. To become a human panacea. All humans on earth are here for a reason to learn and accept a lesson that is unseeably being taught. We are here to do more than drive to McDonalds or shop in malls. We are here to love the ones who adopt hate. We are here to understand each other without the insolent divide that ignorantly sees humans as lesser beings due to the color of one's skin, when it's the contents of one's character that should be sought. We are here to rehabilitate the rehabilitatable. We are to forgive, even if Redemption isn't feasible. We are here to get off our couches and seek for our meanings, our whys in this life and make a difference.

Observation is nine-tenths of the human law, and I've shared what I have observed. If we completely understand self first—then we can understand others—who we are all designed in the same likeness with the same capability to function the exact same. I have come and said my peace. Now I bid you all adieu.

Peace and blessings to all.
Charles "Chucky" Mamou

William Mason
#999040

Age: 54
Hometown: Houston, Texas
Last school: Lee College, Lovelady, Texas
Education: GED *plus one hundred some-odd hours*
Favorites: Movies - The Count of Monte Cristo, Lonesome Dove; *Ice cream - Blue Bell's Chocolate Turtle Fudge; Cars - Harley Davidson or Chevy truck*

Each individual and each race of mankind have special aims. Even though we are not consciously aware of them, these aims have a great effect on our lives, the way we think and the actions we take, each of them personal, individual and indefinable. I made bad choices in my younger years. I could come up with a hundred excuses, but still somewhere down the line we all have to pay the price when you deal in vice, but I say! What is right for me may not be right for you and vice versa. So what is right and what is wrong? Is it right for people to place themselves as the eyes of God? They hear a story told from bits and pieces with the truth hidden behind a bodyguard of lies and judge a fellow man to rot away in a cage awaiting for his number to be called, while all his family and friends die and he's left alone at the mercy of his kids, fresh out of high school, control his every move. People are not naturally bad but the true stories never get told, always sugarcoated.

Peace and love,
Billy Mason

Rodolfo Medrano
#999501

Age: 29
Hometown: Elsa, Texas
Last school: Texas State Technical College, Harlingen, Texas
Education: Associate's degree
Interests: Computers, fishing, sports, Bible studies
Favorites: Ice cream - strawberry sundae with pecans;
            Favorite meal - wife's enchiladas with Mexican rice and beans;
            Fast food - Whataburger with cheese and bacon;
            Fruit - melons
Other info: I am married to my college sweetheart. We have one son and we've
            been married for nine years. I am the third in a family of four. I
            believe Jesus Christ is the Son of God and hold the Bible as the
            only authority for life and conduct. I've been a Christian since 2003.

Capital Punishment in Texas

In Texas, a death sentence is reached by the answers jurors give to the following three questions:

Special Issue No. 1:

Is there a probability that the Defendant would commit criminal acts of violence that would constitute a continuing threat to society?

Special Issue No. 2:

Do you find from the evidence beyond a reasonable doubt that the Defendant himself, actually caused the deaths of the deceased, on the occasion in question, or, if he did not actually cause the death of the deceased, that he intended to kill the deceased or another, or anticipated that a human life would be taken?

Special Issue No. 3:

Whether, taking into consideration all of the evidence, including the circumstances of the offense, the Defendant's character and background, and the personal moral culpability of the Defendant, there is sufficient mitigating circumstance or circumstances to warrant that a sentence of life imprisonment rather than a death sentence be imposed?

The jurors must answer these questions with "yes" or "no" answers. There is only way for a death sentence to be reached, and that is by answering:

Special Issue No. 1 - YES
Special Issue No. 2 - YES
Special Issue No. 3 - NO

Any other combination would result in an automatic life sentence in prison. Life in prison means you must serve at least forty years to be eligible for parole, but does not guarantee you will be given parole by Texas. Texas rarely gives prisoners parole on their parole hearings, meaning you will serve more years before you are given another parole hearing.

Consider this, when a person is sent to prison he must work at least four hours a day. This work is without wages and usually confined to hard labor in the prison fields under harsh weather. A refusal to work results in disciplinary action and even worse, affects the prisoners' next parole hearing. No work, no parole, leaving a prisoner no option but to work, if he desires to leave the prison.

If this truly is about punishment for a crime, would not this life sentence seem more logical? It is about punishment right?

Fortunately, jurors in Texas now have the option of life in prison without the possibility of parole. No hope, no dream, no chance, no opportunity to ever leave prison, ever, and again a life of hard labor in Texas prisons. It is about punishment, right?

Texas' death penalty is reserved for capital murder in all its varying forms. It sought for nineteen different types of murder, but here we will focus on one only. Our focus is on "intentionally or knowingly causing the deaths of more than one person during the same criminal transaction, by shooting them with a firearm" Texas Penal Code §19.02 (b) (1) and §19.03 (7) (A).

I was accused of shooting and killing six people. I was told that I would be facing the death penalty for this crime. I thought to myself, "How can they seek the death penalty against me when I didn't shoot anyone? I wasn't even there when these people were killed."

"Welcome to Texas! And in this corner Texas' undisputed champion, The Law of Parties!!!!" I had never heard of this monster. I thought monsters were make believe, that they lived in books, movies and dreams, but not in Texas. Come to know, I would be facing Texas' monster, The Law of Parties. I am now on death row because of Texas' monster. The District Attorney never disputed the fact that I was never present at the murder scene. The DA never disputed the fact that I never fired a single bullet, let alone killed anyone. The DA never disputed the fact that I spent the late night hours at home, with my wife, watching movies when the crime was committed. Regardless of these facts, the DA believed that I should be given the death penalty for not foreseeing the deaths that occurred, which I did not intend to happen nor cause myself, while these same DAs chose not to seek the death penalty on those that were present at the murder scene. Worse, the DAs released them without any punishment. They believed it was just to seek the harshest punishment Texas has, to sick their monster on me, when I never fired a bullet.

There is no doubt this was a serious crime, but the death penalty is reserved for actual murderers, which I am not, as the evidence proves. The death penalty is an acceptable punishment for murder to most people in Texas, but it surely can't be and shouldn't be acceptable in my case, can it?

Our justice system is set up to punish according to the crime that was actually committed, which is true justice. Texas' Law of Parties states, "all conspirators are GUILTY of the felony actually committed, though having no INTENT to commit it." This is not justice, especially when the DAs pick and choose who they will seek the death penalty on, regardless if they killed anyone. The Law of Parties disregards the basics of our justice system, "punishment according to the crime" when DAs are free to pick and choose who is worthy of death, and who is not, regardless of their actual crime. This monster allowed Hidalgo County District Attorneys to send me to death row, when I did not shoot anyone, while they released those that might have done it.

This is Texas' Monster, the Law of Parties, which district attorneys use to condemn a non-triggerman, a person who did not kill anyone and wasn't even present at the scene. This is what has sent me to death row, not a murder I committed, but one I failed to anticipate. Texas' monster and the DAs and a jury of my "peers" has sentenced me to die for being negligent, while these same DAs released those that were possibly the actual shooters. Is the death sentence a proper punishment for being negligent? Texas and its monster seem to think so. Do you?

YES + YES + NO = DEATH. This is Texas' equation for JUSTICE, and the solution for mere negligence.

Jedidiah Murphy
#999392

Age:　　33
Education:　*Twelfth grade*

There are people who are good at expressing themselves on paper and there are those who are good at doing the same thing in person. I, being one of the latter, don't write too many articles or opinions, but today I'm gonna try and make a good effort at describing something about this place.

There are those who ask what it is like living in a place like this and time and time again I see that description falls short. People tend to concentrate on one aspect of this time and leave the rest to the reader's imagination. Personally I quit trying to sum this place up with words years ago. Some days I think "today I have the words," yet when I put them to paper I realized that was wrong. I don't think you can use words to describe this place the way most people want to know it. It's more of a feeling and that is the hardest thing to transfer to paper.

There is something that floats in the air here that is unlike anything that I have ever seen or felt in my life. It's like going to a funeral service having never met the deceased, yet because of the sense of loss that surrounds the place, YOU TOO begin to feel the same as those who actually knew the person that passed. The big difference between that and this is the apprehension. We all know that our time will come to us here. The exact date is provided to us and that is something the average man will never know. It's that same timeline that drives some of us over the edge of sanity and causes others to drop their appeals so they don't have to deal with years of that feeling.

Our fate lies in the hands of attorneys that most times care very little for us or don't care at all. We have family that pull away from us because they can't stand to see what our time is doing to us and the stress it causes them to come to the unit to see us. This takes a toll on everyone not just the ones here. I've lost contact with people I thought would be in my life forever. I don't think there is a single man here who doesn't have the same story to tell when it comes to that. Wives divorce husbands and take children away with the IDEA that they are doing it for their own good. Family members die as well as friends and all of that is stacked upon the stacks of other things we carry on our shoulders from day to day. Men who came to this place with their backs straight and in good shape begin to look old beyond their years. Death has a weight to it. Not a weight that is felt by the spirit but that takes a toll on the body as well.

We watch friends leave this place and never come back. I've reached a point where I don't seek friends anymore. I know that one day I'll have to see them take that walk and lose them to a flawed system in the name of JUSTICE. This time changes everyone in some way or the other. For some it takes years for that change to manifest itself but sooner or later it will show itself. It makes men who were evil to become good. It also makes a man who was once passive become aggressive and lash out of frustration and anger. Most of us had some sort of personality problem that led us to drugs and that same glitch along with the new stress that we are exposed to here will cause many a man to lose his mind altogether.

I and everyone in this section just watched them take an inmate out in the van that will take him to the execution chamber in Huntsville. He is a friend of mine. I've known him since I came to Death Row. Now I know I will never see him again and that is something I've gone through many times here. All I can do is put my fist to the window and show him some respect and turn around. He's one less friend I'll have come six o'clock this afternoon. This place will pick back up to its usual pace and the day will go on as if nothing really happened outside that window. That's how it's done here.

I was told a minute ago that they had to run in on four people. That was done to show them that they are killing a human being and not just a number. Do you remember the last good friend that you lost? Can you imagine what it is like to lose three to four in a single year? That's what it is like here year after year. Once again, these words don't come close to what I feel inside or come close to what this place is truly like. I don't think I'll ever be able to get it down on paper properly. I'll keep trying though as a form of therapy for myself. I'll leave you with this for now because I want to sit back and think about what I just saw outside my little window. It's not easy to watch a man walk to his death . . . what do you think it was like for the man who did the walking?

Julius Murphy
#999279

Age: 30
Hometown: Texarkana, Texas
Last school: Nichols Junior High, Arlington, Texas
Education: Seventh grade
Interests: Reading comic books, working out, reading, and writing
Favorites: Cars - Chevrolet, Cadillac, GMC; Movies - X-Files *(both TV show and movies),* Jean Claude Van-Damme movies; Ice cream - mint chocolate chip, chocolate chip cookie dough; Books - Stephen King books

Roderick Newton
#999348

Age: *30*
Hometown: *Dallas, Texas*
Last school: *Skyline High School, Dallas, Texas*
Education: *Tenth grade*
Interests: *I want to write books that appeal to masses.*
Favorites: *Books* - Brother Ray: Ray Charles' Own Story, Crime
     Pays; *Author - Tha Twinz; Movie -* King of New York;
     Ice cream - rocky road; Cars - Lexus, Caddy, Corvette, Nissan
     Pathfinder

It's not known why things happen as they do? Sometimes things just happen for the good. Sometimes things happen for the bad. But however or whatever happens, a person must be ready to deal with it. Whether it be a hurricane, earthquake, loss of an loved one, wrongly convicted, or simply a flat tire. The best thing anyone can do is always be prepared for the good, as well as for the bad. If one stays ready, then the time will never come when you would be placed in the position of getting ready. You'll never miss a good thing until it's gone. I have been to so many funerals and witnessed people feeling guilty. They have to carry the heavy burden as they have reflected towards the way they treated someone before they pass on.

As I grew and matured, I have learned never to take for granted friendships, and the people dear to my heart, and always try to love as if there is no tomorrow for they could be here today and gone tomorrow.

So ask yourself this question? Are you ready?

Salute,
Roderick

Abel Ochoa
#999450

Age: 35
Hometown: Dallas
Last school: Sunset High School, Dallas, Texas
Education: Twelfth grade
Interests: Writing letters and reading spiritual books
Favorites: Book - Karla Faye Tucker's Set Free
Other info: I believe, as humans, we all need friendship and
            companionship, and I personally seek both.

My name is Abel R. Ochoa, and unfortunately I am writing from Death Row. What got me into this horrible place? My addiction to smoking crack. I was first introduced to it by *so-called* friends (real friends don't introduce you to drugs), around early 2000. I started off using little by little, but as time went on, the amounts increased until finally, I was addicted to it.

Why would I smoke crack? I was looking for peace, due to the different problems I was having in my life. Smoking crack would allow my mind to escape reality for a few hours, depending on the amount I smoked.

That "temporary peace" the drug would give me by escaping reality for a few hours, I would find out later was a "false-peace." By God's grace I know true, everlasting peace, that only comes through His only begotten Son Jesus Christ. God showed me through the Holy Spirit that the peace I sought in the form of drugs, was a lie of satan, who Jesus called in the Bible, "The father of all lies."

Many brothers I have met here on the Row have shared with me similar experiences. They sought "peace" in their lives, to escape problems in their lives, and sought it out in the form of different drugs. For me personally, the day of my arrest, I smoked crack and within a few minutes, lives were taken, due to a "drug induced delirium" as concluded by a doctor who examined a CAT scan done on my brain, and as well spoke with me on my drug-usage, and examined my past life.

Now I sit here on the Row waiting for the laws of man to execute me. What's it like here in a ten-by-seven cell, waiting to get executed? I'm at peace, real peace, which surpasses all human understanding. Eternal peace that only comes though the Holy Spirit. If you are reading this, I would encourage you to never try drugs. They don't give you any kind of peace; it is a lie from satan. If you know someone on drugs, reach out to them and tell them that God loves them and wants to give them the peace that surpasses all understanding.

May God bless you all,
Abel R. Ochoa

Ker'Sean Ramey
#999519

Age: 23
Hometown: *Victoria, Texas*
Last school: *Edna High School, Edna, Texas*
Education: *Eleven and a half*
Interests: *Animals, reading, poetry, understanding more*
Favorites: Book - The Female Brain *by Louann Brizendine; Movie -* Love and Basketball*; Ice cream - butter pecan*

     I'm Ker'Sean Ramey, a twenty-three year old (June 4, 1985) Black male on Texas Death Row. I was twenty-one upon my arrival, very hurt and aggravated. I was hurt to see those who I've helped, loved, saved, supported, and encouraged turn their backs on me at a critical moment in my life. How can someone I've given a place to stay turn on me you ask . . . good question. Who would turn and lie on someone who loved them and would "die" for them you ask? Even better question. But I have no answers for you and those questions, only deep scars and papers stained with the tears I've shed on sleepless nights.

     I was aggravated because I found out there is no such thing as true JUSTICE in Texas! If you have money, you can say you did anything and "still" get away with it. But if you are poor, you honestly do not have a chance—even if you are "innocent." I was aggravated because I was taken away from my family against my will like a slave for a crime I not only did not commit, but had another man tell the jurors: "he did it," not me. My prosecutor told the jury to "ASSUME" that I used a gun to commit this crime. My "LIFE" is on the line and he's giving jurors instructions to use ASSUMPTIONS, to "assume" that I used a gun!! They may as well have told them to "assume" I'm guilty too.

     Thus these are some of the reasons I was hurt and aggravated when I arrived here. Everything I've said, I can show anyone who's interested on paper, I haven't fabricated anything. So, being here for a crime I didn't commit and being a wild twenty-one year old youngster didn't mix too well. I didn't know how to control my emotions in the slightest way. I would get mad because the officers would do things to me and they wouldn't be following the rules but if "I" didn't follow them, I'd get in trouble.

I don't believe that just because they wear gray suits that makes them better than me, no. So I'd be quick to tell them whatever I felt, however I felt, whenever I felt … I'd be the only one to stand up and say something, then I started to see "some" others start standing up for themselves as well. Then the officers would say, you're (I am) bad or rebellious, cause you stand up for yourself and others don't. But sometimes I would go off and cuss the officers out for anything like staring at me. I just couldn't control my emotions and I couldn't stand law enforcement personnel period because of my experience with them during my trial. The way they did me when my life was on the line, they showed me they didn't care about me (a peer), guilt or innocence, or justice for that matter, so the feeling became mutual.

Some of the old school cats would try and calm me down and steer me in the right direction, but it wasn't my time and you can't teach someone something who "thinks" they already know it all. A officer told me one time that she would help me pass some magazines I had for someone. I looked at her like she was crazy or from another planet, and said no, I'll do it myself. Because of my bad experience with my "so-called" friends, I didn't feel I could trust "anyone" but the people who were there for me when I needed them, which weren't many.

This continued until I started to put my feelings on paper, in poems. This was very therapeutic to me and it helped to settle my aggravation at the bottom, but now the hurt had surfaced again. When I write I'm very emotional, I speak directly from the heart. So now I wasn't cussing and going off on officers, I simply wouldn't talk to them at all.

Then on July 4, 2007, I was writing and my neighbor said look out the window—I didn't even know it was the fourth of July. I looked and saw a bunch of different colors and styles of colorful fireworks; it was beautiful. Then I started to think about me missing out on popping fireworks with my babies, and I suddenly got this knot in my stomach and I got down and went to sleep. After that I covered up my window and didn't uncover it for over a year. I would be sad for a while then it would turn back into aggravation and the cycle continued.

Until one day, someone asked me to hold some books for them

because they had too many and I said yes. I got them and glanced at the covers then placed them under my bunk's locker. From time to time I'd look at the covers again, but I was really bored this day and decided to read the summary on the back of one of the books. It seemed interesting, so I had nothing else to do, why not, I opened the book up and commenced to read it.

It was a spiritual book, and I felt what it was saying, and I read the whole book. After that, I started to like reading only spiritual books, then I graduated to psychology and so on. Through reading I've learned more than I ever did in school and I've grown to a new way of thinking, talking and living. I'm nowhere near "perfect" but I'm nowhere near what I "used" to be either. And I'm very proud of myself for my achievements. I'm living proof that anyone who "wants" to can change.

If you go look at a tree in the "winter," you see an ugly, bent, withered, twisted tree. And I go see it in the summer and I see a beautiful tree with green buds all over it. We both saw the same tree just at different seasons in the tree's life. You can't judge the tree by just the winter season, cause then you'd miss out on the beauty it brings in the summer. In life we may have difficult seasons, but if you push and preserve through it, better times are sure to come. Even though it's hard to see through the darkness, just remember, it takes darkness to see the stars. . . .

Sincerely,
Ker'Sean Ramey

Martin Robles
#999457

Age: 30
Hometown: *Corpus Christi, Texas*
Last school: *Black Stone Career Institute*
Education: *GED/paralegal*
Interests: *Women, music, law, politics, reading and writing, exercising, space, history*
Favorites: *Book - the Bible; Color - blue; Movie -* Gladiator*; Shoes - Nike; Ice cream - banana split; Actor - Al Pacino; Cars - Ferrari, Lamborghini; Actress - all women; Beer - Budweiser; Liquor - Jack Daniels, Crown Royal; Soft drink - root beer, Sprite; Foods - seafood, all food; Dress shoes - Stacy Adams; Truck/SUV - Lincoln Navigator, Cadillac Escalade; Sports - basketball, football*

By the time you read these words, I will be exonerated from Death Row. I will also be publishing my own book and creating music as well as capitalizing on my experiences in prison as well as my experiences on death row in order to generate revenue for charitable causes. So if you are wondering, then yes I'm here to tell you that I'm a Christian.

As a child I was raised Roman Catholic but no longer support its system due to scripture. When I say I want you to know, it is not my intention to offend anyone, so don't feel that way when you hear or read something about me or by me. I give my effort to approach everyone as a friend because it is the best way to gain the favor of the people. My main goal is to convert everyone into representing the Church of Christ. The story I want to share with you today though is the day I was nearly killed. None of what I say is false. This really happened and there are not many who can do what I do. In the Bible it says: "Have faith in God," Matthew 11:22, and that is exactly how I live my life.

May 24, 2002 was a Friday and my childhood friends and I would barbeque, drink, watch movies, and play billiards. We would shoot dice and gamble, go cruising and have fun. It was a "couple" thing where the guys would bring their female friends to form friendships. On this particular Friday I went to the convenience store to buy beer, snacks, and soft drinks with my girlfriend and her daughters. She was driving. I was on the passenger seat and her daughters were in the back seat. When we pulled up to the store, I gave her some money to buy what was needed and stayed in the car as she went inside with her daughters. As I sat in the car, I started fooling around with the radio and some guys rolled up next to me. Ordinarily you would think these were peaceful citizens and that's why I wasn't paying attention. I was in my community, my "hood" so to speak and frequented this store many times growing up. I had no reason to be cautious, so when my female friend got back in the car with her daughters she asked me a simple question, "Why are those guys looking at you?"

Normally a person might think these guys were gay since there were no women in the car and they might be, who really knows? All I knew is that when I looked out the window, I saw a bunch of guys looking at me. I've always had this problem. You can call it "envy," "jealousy," and straight up "hate" for me. Being the handsome fellow that I am, it comes with the territory.

Anyway, I realized something violent was going to happen. I could tell by the faces they were making. It was eight of them and one of me. Not fair for them since I'm a pretty good fighter when I want to be. After I sized up my competition I told my female friend, "I don't know, but I'm going to use the bathroom."

I got off the car. That's right, I got off the car. That's how real I am. If you thought I was going to stay in the car, you're mistaken. Being a coward has never been in my blood unlike others may have heard about. I got off the car so I could give my female friend a chance to leave the scene with her daughters before the bullets started flying.

I said, "what's up" and as I entered the store, one of them said, "That's him." That's right, I'm him and in this type of situation a person has to think fast because not only is his safety on the line but the safety of others. Since there were customers everywhere, I walked into the bathroom to relieve myself and hoped my female friend left the scene. No such luck! I then looked in the mirror, smiled, laughed softly and told myself, "now I'm gonna die" and walked out. My friend's daughter was at the cashier counter with that look on her face that said don't go outside. She was scared and she had a right to be. She was a fifteen year old child at that time and I told her, "Don't worry; everything's going to be alright."

When I stepped outside the door, the shooter raised his hand and I saw the gun. He then said something and I raised my hands and said something. I didn't have anything nice to say, so I won't write it down. But you can use your imagination. A group of them attacked me with very poor skills in hand to hand combat. After I defended myself and slapped a few around like women, they stepped back and proceeded to group around their leader with the gun. I then walked away from my friend's car. I didn't want the shooter shooting at the car so I directed the attention towards me. Am I a real hero or what? It's the main reason I got off the car in the first place so that the people I was with wouldn't be hurt.

As I was walking away from the car, the shooter had his gun pointed at me. We weren't that far apart—maybe twenty feet. Seconds felt like minutes and I never took my eyes off the man who shot and tried to kill me. I wanted to attack him but there were too many plus they had a gun and all I had was a few hundred dollars in my pocket, my gold necklace and bracelet plus my Nike shoes and clothes I was wearing.

Throughout the whole experience I kept my cool. I raised my arms and said "shoot" and he shot me at the same time I said it. The first bullet hit my right forearm. I was surprised it didn't hit me in the face or chest since the shooter was pointing the gun directly at me. I looked at my forearm, saw the bullet hole and became very angry. I raised my left hand to point at him and said, "I got you baby." I then proceeded to run and the shooter unloaded a 9mm clip. Boom, boom, boom, boom, boom that struck me a few times.

I fell down in front of a house and was able to tell the people who were sitting down outside to call an ambulance. They seemed scared since they saw me fall.

The churches of Christ salute you and thank you for giving me this opportunity to showcase my mind.

Your Saint in Christ Jesus,
Martin Robles

Rosendo Rodriguez, III
#999534

Age: 28
Hometown: *Wichita Falls, Texas*
Last school: *Texas Tech University, Lubbock, Texas*
Education: *Junior in college*
Interests: *Soccer, football, Democratic politics, military history, Dungeons and Dragons*
Favorites: *Books -* The Ruins *by Scott Smith,* The Road *by Cormac McCarthy; Movies -* Pulp Fiction, Gladiator; *Magazines -* Time, Rolling Stone; *Actors - Christopher Walken, Martin Sheen*
Other info: *Having traveled a lot both with my family and with the Marines during my service, I would like for those who read my submission to know that nowhere else have I ever met a more intelligent, free thinking group of individuals as I have here in prison on Death Row. I wrote my submission to let people know that there are people worthy of redemption and a chance to rehabilitate.*

Hello, my name is Rosendo Rodriguez, III, and I thank you for the submission request. I myself attended college at Texas Tech, and I was a double major (Political Science and History) with a minor in English.

I am an engaging conversationalist and I promise not to disappoint.

On May 14, 2008, I arrived on Death Row here on the Polunsky Unit in Livingston, Texas. I would like for people to know that there are people here who are imprisoned, who despite public opinion, maintain an overall sense of basic human kindness and compassion. Hopefully my words may dispel some misconceptions of those who have never visited or experienced a place such as this.

During a thunderstorm, in the mid-afternoon, I was brought to the Byrd unit in Huntsville for diagnostic and processing. Since I was to become a Death Row inmate, I was expedited through the usual process normally reserved for all non-death sentenced offenders. Those other inmates who had been waiting hours, perhaps even days, had to wait even longer as I was issued clothing, given a Concentration-Camp style haircut and shave, then taken to the administrative offices for the inevitable bureaucratic nightmare of paperwork. As I was questioned about my Marine eagle, globe, and anchor tattoo, cold indifference then gave way to lukewarm friendliness. Several administrative staff as well as correctional officers began to talk about their own military service, or the service of friends and family members.

I began to notice that I was increasingly becoming engaged in conversation more befitting a bar or café type atmosphere, rather than a man condemned to death while sitting inside of a prison. When I was fingerprinted by a kind matronly woman, she asked if I bit my nails, which is a habit I've never been able to break. When photographed, several of the female office workers tried to get me to laugh or smile for the camera. I maintained an impassive face and stoic bearing, for I knew that deep down, there would be a point in which all the friendliness and lighthearted banter would disappear, and the hard reality of life in the system would finally hit.

I was then brought to the Polunsky Unit in a prison van, in an ever increasing downpour. The van driver, having more testicular fortitude than brains, as well as NASCAR aspirations, took it upon himself to drive eighty-five miles per hour, negotiating curves with reckless abandon through the torrential rain. How ironic it would be, I thought, jostling around in the back of the speeding, swinging van, to escape the executioner's needle, only to meet a more conventional, vehicular demise. The Wheels of Justice however, were not frustrated by the wheels of a prison van, and I arrived at my new (and possibly last) residence.

Ironically, the rain stopped as soon as we arrived, as if to say "Here, take a good look, we would not want you to miss a thing." The sense of the dramatic was not lost on either Mother Nature, nor the architect of the prison. Armed guards with rifles stood sentry atop towers at intersections of ten-foot fences topped with razor wire. I half expected to see a large wrought-iron sign with the words "ARBEIT MACHT FREI" (the sign which hung above the entryway of the Treblinka death camp in Nazi-occupied Poland). I did see however the words "ALAN B. POLUNSKY UNIT DEATH ROW" on a wall, proudly adorned with the Texas flag and state seal, so I suppose it all evened out.

After walking into the building with the sign, I was taken to the infirmary for a rudimentary physical, and questions about my medical history. I was slightly offended at being told I weighed 198 pounds; they obviously did not take into account the padlock, chains and cuffs used to restrain my movement. A dental exam and x-rays were provided. (I was informed I had good teeth). I was then deemed fit enough for their needs and brought before the captain, major, and warden for classification. This part of the process was probably the most strict, as I was repeatedly asked why I was here at Death Row. Because I did not feel the need to tell them what they probably already knew, I respectfully declined to answer. This did not sit well. But legally I had no reason to speak of why I was convicted, and they knew this as well.

So instead, they ordered me to strip in front of them as well as other correctional officers and staff of both sexes, which in my mind was their attempt to humiliate me or break my spirit. But as I had to do the same in front of many people while being processed at Marine boot camp, I had no reason to feel embarrassed. Satisfied that I had no other tattoos, they told me to put my clothes on and I was then taken to my cell.

Humans have landed probes on Mars, cloned animals, harnessed the power of the atom to power our Megacities, and have connected globally via the internet. Yet we cannot process a simple ID card in less than three weeks. You see, an ID card in prison allows an inmate to go to visits, buy various sundry items like hygiene, or foodstuffs, etc. So when you first arrive, you are not able to buy the basic things you need like a plastic spoon or cup or shampoo, until you receive your card. Inmates understand this, and the inmates here on Death Row do help each other with this concern. Thirty minutes after entering my cell, the feeding tray slot in my door opened and several packages of instant soups, bags of chips, letter writing supplies, stamps, basic hygiene items, were pushed through.

I knew that then it wasn't going to be as bad as I had heard. If there was something I would like the outside world to know, it is that human kindness and decency exists here. In the midst of what the State of Texas has deemed the worst of the system, so terrible that we cannot be a part of and congregate with and like the general population, so feared that we have to be executed, prisoners of Death Row exhibit compassion and a need to help those who are in the same position.

Someone, I forget who, (and I am probably paraphrasing this badly as well) wrote "Death is the greatest democratizer." As we all face the same sentence, the spectre of death constantly hanging over our head, it will foster a modicum of respect between inmates here.

Since Death Row prisoners are not allowed to congregate or have contact (you're handcuffed everywhere you go, and kept with at least some barrier between you) you get to know one another by shouting from cell to cell, or from whatever dayroom you are in. Sports, politics, family situations, penpal situations, and outside world life experiences (whether true or not) tend to dominate most conversations. I would also like people in the outside world to know that some of the most amiable and intelligent people I've ever met have been the ones I've come across while incarcerated. I've been to college, traveled on my own as well as in the military, and nowhere else have I ever met such outgoing and interesting people.

Now I do realize that all of us here have been accused (keyword accused) of capital murder, and I am not trying to make light of this, nor am I trying to paint this place as a "We-are-the-World-Everyone-joins-hands-and-sings-Kumbayah" type of environment. Constant cell searches, inconsistent and ever changing rules, a few overzealous guards and staff, and the general monotony of everyday rigmarole adds to stress and anxiety that we already endure.

But I am thoroughly convinced that if many of the proponents of the death penalty actually saw how relatively docile Death Row really is, and with the tact and respect of how we prisoners treat each other and the guards and staff, then many of the pro-death penalty advocates would be inclined to take a moment of reflective pause. All of us here have lives that are salvageable, lives that are redeemable, lives worth knowing about. This place was not as bleak as I'd imagined, and I'm sure that if more people took the time to contact us, to see how our lives really are rather than how some prosecutor or pro-death organization portrays it to be, I'm sure that many people would see it the way I do.

Vaughn Ross
#999429

Age: *37*
Hometown: *Saint Louis, Missouri*
Last school: *Texas Tech University, Lubbock, Texas*
Education: *College graduate (BS and AS degrees)*
Interests: *Learning new things, travel, and living life to the fullest*
Other info: *Personal philosophy is knowledge is key to a life of enjoyment and opens many doors of opportunity.*

A Theory for an Execution

There are many theories in society to explain those things that we just do not know or have not witnessed. Such theories are The Big Bang, Creationism and The Theory of Evolution.

In my first example, The Big Bang is a cosmological theory that the universe and all creation therein it originated approximately ten to fifteen billion years ago from the violent eruption of a very small mass of hot, dense matter.

Whereas Creationism accounts for the same theory is what is literally told in the Book of Genesis. In that theory God created the heavens, the earth and all things in six days. And related to that we have the Theory of Evolution where it is believed that man and other species gradually changed over time from organisms into a different and better or more complex form in some cases. With this theory each phase of change has not been discovered or accounted for. Which one of these theories is true? That all depends on what you believe and put your trust in.

According to *Webster's Dictionary*, theory is defined as: systematically organized knowledge applicable in a relatively wide variety of circumstances, especially a system of assumptions, accepted principles, and rules of procedure devised to analyze, predict or otherwise explain the nature or behavior of a specified set of phenomenon. What may be my fate was decided on this definition of theory.

On September 23, 2002, I was convicted of the capital murder of two people during the same criminal transaction. The conviction was based on a theory presented by the prosecutor to a so-called jury of my peers. None of the jurors were of my race, age or background. After a few brief hours of deliberation the next day I was sentenced to die by lethal injection.

The state's theory that was presented during trial was not based on eyewitness testimony, facts or direct evidence. In fact, it was based on circumstantial evidence and a gut feeling the prosecutor had of my guilt. My life was judged, weighed and decided not worthy to live in a week's amount of time. Ultimately taken from me based on a hunch one man had. This was even after he admitted that he did not know what happened in the case. All that was known for sure is that two people had been killed and I was the chosen one to be held responsible for the crime. If this does not appall you add to it the fact that the state offered a life plea bargain. To get death in a capital offense one must prove beyond a reasonable doubt that the convicted will be a future danger to society. Or did the state not want to take the case to trial and have to prove its theory and incur the cost of litigation? I have my own theories on that. In the end we will not know the truth of the matter until all facts are revealed. Something that may never come to light.

There are many like me on death row whose fates have been decided not by our own actions, but on the perceived thoughts or theories of others for heinous acts committed against the peace and dignity of society. A theory should not be accepted as a means to facilitate the murder of a human being. Especially not when the theory cannot be proven. Some things we cannot prove and will not know the truth of its origins or details of the event that brought it about. In my case the state knew it had a weak case with no proof, so it created A Theory for an Execution. The facts did not add up to my guilt of committing such a crime. Someone had to pay for the crime as I was told by the lead detective, so an acceptable explanation was devised on limited information to be analyzed by the jury. Just like the infamous Theory of Evolution, there were missing links unexplained or assumed to have happened to win a conviction or convince the jury.

During biblical times, the innocent were sacrificed for the crimes and sins of the community. Are we still practicing these rituals today with the enforcement of capital punishment under an eye for an eye? You tell me. Maybe it's just a theory of mine that needs to be proven.

Travis Runnels
#999505

Age: *32*
Hometown: Dallas
Last school: Skyline High School, Dallas, Texas
Education: Ninth grade
Interests: Psychology, history, and nature

Destiny

When you look at your life do you have a destiny or plan? What is your life to you? What is your purpose on this earth? Is it to work every day and go home to your family or is there a reason that you are living and breathing? Could be so simple that you were born just to work every day until you die and accomplish nothing worthy or helpful to others?

Sit back and take a look at your life and ask yourself, why do I get up every morning? Am I a difference maker in this world or am I just here living for my own selfish reasons? If I die today, in what way would my life have affected those around me? Is there something I accomplished that my family could be proud of or will they just be sad that I'm no longer living? What can my kids tell people about me to where you can hear the pride in their voice, or will they just be proud to talk about me only because I am their parent? How much intelligence does it take to become a parent? Are there only certain people who can do this or can anyone do it? So how can your kids be proud of something anyone with sexual organs can accomplish with a minimal of effort?

Think about yourself and what it is you think you need and want out of life besides making money to pay bills, and getting the things you need. What have I done that will help others better themselves? Why am I living without a purpose in life? My life is a special one, my life is a worthy one that people will envy because, I will live for the well being for those around me. I'm not perfect but I want to understand why people are put into this world or why we exist in the universe. Are we here just to live and then die for no other purpose? Could it be that simple but yet we are built with so much intelligence and understanding? What is my mind for, what are my thoughts for? For daydreaming or can they be for achieving great things for the world that I live and exist in?

So I must start to understand and get a better idea of myself and those around me. Then we can help each other come to the same idea of what we all stand for. There has to be a common ground among us of what life stands for and means. I reach into the inner depths of your consciousness and seek out the truth of understanding for your peace of mind. What you come to understand, then share with those around you. Always remember life is what you make of it and you can accomplish nothing without using your mind.

Come Live With Me

Once the handcuffs are placed on, you take a ride in a police car. Then when you get to jail you're placed in a holding pen where it feels like it's twenty degrees. There is a crowd of men cramped into this place, some dirty and filthy, some are drunk and the whole place smells of urine. As you look for a place to sit there is none. The only option is the floor. You choose to stand so you can better think about how you got into this situation and what you're gonna do to get out of it. You know in your mind this is gonna be the hardest test you've ever faced. As you feel around in your pockets only a few coins move around. Then you think about having to fight the system without money and depend on overworked and underfunded court appointed lawyers to help you.

You instantly take a seat when you realize the hopelessness of your situation. Who can you call for help as you look at the phones. Grandma is poor and living off retirement, mom is an alcoholic and dad is not around. Friends are out of the question because they are the reason you're in this cell now. After sitting or standing for most of the day a guard comes in and calls about five names of those to come with him. Your name is one of them so you get up and follow.

He leads you to a room with a bunch of shelves with laundry on them. Once inside he tells everyone to strip out of all their clothes and put them in a bag he gives you. As you're all standing naked the guard tells you to raise your privates up, then turn around and spread your buttocks. Now pick one foot up at a time. Once this humiliation is finished he gives everyone a jail jumpsuit and a pair of boxers. He then throws each of you a laundry roll which consist of boxers, socks, towel, sheets, blanket and toilet paper. You are told not to lose these things because they will have to be turned back in. Whatever you don't have you will be charged for. He walks out and says follow me where he takes you to get a mattress. Then you are walked to where you will be housed until your court date. He calls out your name to go in this section with twenty-four bunks inside. In front of you are tables occupied by men who all turn to look at you. There are two phones right next to the door and one has a guy on it who's screaming at someone to come and get him out. The TV is sky high. In each sleeping area you can see people loitering around, clothes hanging up and newspaper over lights to give it a night club look. Your eyes take all this in a few seconds.

As you walk toward the sleeping area with your measly property you can feel numerous sets of eyes on you with judgment and prejudices. What did he do, is he gay, is he weak, does he have money? When you walk in toward a bunk three sets of eyes instantly meet yours, you ignore the looks and go to the empty bunk in the back. Throw your things down and get settled in because this is where you will live, eat and breathe until your fate is decided by the judicial system.

As you stand by your bunk unfolding your linens, all types of things are running through your mind, "How did I get in this mess?" You turn around because now it's time to meet the men you will be living with for twenty-four hours a day. The guy on the wall says his name and asks if you need a cup and spoon because he has extra. You say yes, your name is Travis and you both nod your heads. The other two sitting on their beds are [names withheld]. You start telling them you are in for robbery and they tell you to be careful, guys have been going to court getting big time for robbery. This makes you feel worse because you know you will have a court-appointed lawyer.

You walk to the door of the cell and as you're looking at all the guys sitting you realize what you're seeing. People watching TV, playing table games or working out. Probably all of those guys have court appointed lawyers, yet their attention is focused on things that are irrelevant to their freedom. As you go jump on your bunk to lay and think all you can do is hope for the best in a hopeless situation.

The days go by and before long you find yourself a part of the distractions the jail offers you. When a lawyer finally decides to visit, it's a lady who's all smiles and feminine charm. Instantly she's talking about some kind of plea deal. You just look at her as if she's insane. You tell her you're not pleading guilty because you're not trying to assure yourself a trip to prison. She is all smiles as she says "you could end up with a lot more time at a trial." Sorry no can do, you'll take your chances with a jury. Now she is ready to leave because she can't get you to bend to her will. You head back to your cell with this consuming your mind because you didn't find out anything specific about your charge. As months and months pass you see men come and go, some home, some to prison. Sitting and waiting because this is the game lawyers and the prosecutors play for those who will not accept plea deals. Finally, after over a year of waiting, your brother says he can get you a lawyer so now you have high hopes of going home. When you first visit with the new lawyer you have doubts instantly about his competence. You know he couldn't have charged much because your brother didn't have much money. So he tells you not to worry; he will win the case. You took his words but didn't put too much faith in them.

Well from day one of the jury trial, things were a disaster. This lawyer was the definition of incompetent. Then to top it off the lawyer gets sick in the middle of the trial and has to be hospitalized for a week. After this is over the jury is in a hurry to get this over and takes little time convicting you. Seventy years in prison. They had the option to choose between fifteen and ninety-nine years. You couldn't believe what you've just heard, your life is over. You are sick to the stomach and have lost all respect for the judicial system. There can be no understanding because it's just been proven it doesn't matter if you're guilty or not.

THE END!

Tarus Sales
#999446

Age: 29
Hometown: *Nashville, Tennessee*
Last school: *Glencliff High, Nashville, Tennessee*
Education: *I dropped school in the ninth grade; however, I received my GED in '98.*
Interests: *One word - "Elite"*
Favorites: Book - Impression *by Krista Johns; Ice cream - vanilla (only with freshly made brownies or baked cookies); Cars - all foreign-born/engineered; Movies -* Belly, Blood Sport, Children of the Corn, The Lion King, Forrest Gump, Titanic

Tarus Speaks

I'm very thankful to have this opportunity to say a few words to the world.

It's difficult to know where to begin as it is difficult to sum up a journey in a few words, and most certainly that is what this death row experience has been. I think it's important to recognize the beauty in those of you who take the time to read this dire message. You must realize that you all have separated and elevated yourselves above the majority of the world. We now live in a spiteful, condemning and quick-to-judge society. Where ruling with an iron fist is more common than an understanding heart.

I've read and heard it said that: "Discretion shall preserve thee, and understanding shall keep thee"; "If you want to know what a society is like, look inside its prisons "; "There are good societies however, a perfect one is impossible with humans being the carpenters of society." To me, those inserts mean that being educated/wise in decision-making and having an understanding heart toward your fellow humans will keep us not revengeful, warring and killing. For no human-doing society or prison is perfect.

My point is that, I believe, "Society and prison are interrelated" and those of you taking the time to read this book hopefully will become people of understanding and decide to listen to the cry of man. The cry of the imprisoned is not always just, but if you never listen to it, you will never know what true justice or injustice is.

So I'm very thankful for your compassion and I know that due to the propaganda propagated by sensationalized media, men on the row are depicted as low-down, sexually deprived, unfeeling, game-playing criminals. Granted, that every prison has its handful of game-players, its psychologically disturbed who don't belong in society in their state of psychosis, its guilty who are remorseful, a few who are not, and its innocent. For the most part, the majority of the row are honest, down-to-earth guys who are undergoing internal transitions as we seek our existential relevance. In doing so we are realists who seek truth irregardless of how difficult it may be to swallow, and many of us fear being exploited and played with as many of us have been exploited by those who seek to capitalize on our difficulties for financial gain. So as concerned as people are out there of being "gamed," vice versa with us in here.

When our world is in a crisis right now, and I have come to the conclusion that it is a spiritual one. Regardless of what your spiritual/religious beliefs are we all have a connection to each other, and that is the inner-substance that binds us all. For some of us on death row we've come to find this substance in a deeper way. Through the (single-man) restrictions and oppression of our five senses we have come to discover a deeper sense with us, and it has been this substance that has carried us through this trying time. The government has said that this is impossible. They have said that we are unable to reform or transform our lives, but anyone who knows me, knows better. You would think that once a system has been proven wrong a more adept one would be installed. That has been the case here. The evidence available shows that the death penalty is not used for what they say, but is in fact a weapon, a tool of attack and revenge calling for human sacrifice.

I, like many others, am a prime example. My situation will stand as a strong contradiction to everything the death penalty says it is about. You see, this system has said that the death penalty shall be saved for the most heinous crime. However, it is a known fact that not a scintilla of evidence links me to this crime, that I did not commit this crime (let alone a heinous crime). Sounds impossible, doesn't it? Well, this is very much a reality in the U.S. There is nothing sensible or righteous about this process. Now with over 140 innocent men and women released from death row and consistent exposure of corruption in the system, Americans are finally waking up to what is really going on. Many have supported the death penalty simply out of ignorance, followers following the crowd. Those of you with the courage to stand up for a just cause have always been the conscience of America. I pray that all of you, those who share the spirit of shedding light on the darkness that this country is facing.

As Dr. Martin Luther King, Jr. once said: "You can't put out darkness with darkness, only light can do that." While I could say much more I just want to thank you for your time and contribution—and I want you all to know that you are serving a just cause for the betterment of humanity.

Case Summary (Submitted by Tarus Sales Himself)

Tarus was "WRONGFULLY CONVICTED" of capital murder as an accomplice and masterminding the fatal retaliation attack of a security guard.

From an unrecorded phone confession—which the full extent of the phone conversation will never be known—between Sgt. [name withheld] (HPD) and [name withheld], who never even testifies: But the sergeant, in his arrest warrant, claims [name withheld] implicates her boyfriend as knowing the true nature of the crime. And based solely on statements made by [name withheld], who also never even testifies, and his life-long friend, [name withheld] is then arrested.

[name withheld], after being arrested and investigated for the murder of the security guard, in the hopes of proving his innocence and cast-iron alibi, implicates Tarus and others telling the police that he knows where the murder weapon is and that he used his personal ID to purchase Tarus an airline ticket the morning of. (The murder weapon was never found! And no ticket was every recorded or subpoenaed!)

When computer evidence showed that the security guard was listed as a state's witness against Tarus for an unrelated deadly conduct charge, police simply took this as motive to wrongfully convict Tarus after they began building a fabricated case against Tarus although not a scintilla of evidence whatsoever links Tarus to the crime.

The prosecution's witnesses were comprised of nothing but a well-known jailhouse snitch and paid Drug Enforcement Agency informant who alleged Tarus confided and confessed to the crime along with another man accused of the same crime before Tarus. Due to no physical evidence linking Tarus to the crime, this is the only way prosecutors tried to place Tarus at the scene—getting and paying a DEA confidential informant and a complete stranger Tarus had never seen nor spoken to a day in his life to lie on Tarus. (For full info. see the State of Texas v. Tarus Vandell Sales Cause No. 893161).

The false testimony, along with the fact that no murder weapon or flight record was ever recovered, no physical evidence links Tarus to the crime, bewilderingly somehow convinced a jury to find Tarus guilty of a crime he never committed. Days later Tarus is shockingly sentenced to murder by lethal injection. THIS INJUSTICE MUST BE STOPPED! THIS INNOCENT MAN, FATHER AND SON MUST BE SAVED!

2-finger (peace), love, and justice
Tarus Sales

Anthony Shore
#999488

Age: 46
Hometown: Houston, Texas since 1981 (born in Rapid City, South Dakota)
Last school: Houston Community College
Education: Some college, no degree
Interests: Music, art, literature, politics, history
Favorites: Movie - Bladerunner; Book - Life of Pi; Song - "Love
            Will Come to You" by Indigo Girls; Memories - Both of my
            daughters!
Other info: Music is in my heart and soul, my first love in life, and it defines
            what and who I am . . . always has! I am a musician and artist. I
            have done many things, but music and art are who I am.

Dance, Sing, Laugh, Be Merry!

I have never been afraid of dying particularly. I have always kind
of just lived life on the edge, searching for the next adrenaline rush
so-to-speak. You see I do believe it is important to plan for the future,
work hard and all that, but know that it is far more important to live
a bit along the way. Life is so very fragile. Take it from someone who
knows. Live as if there is no tomorrow, cause you just never know.

Unfortunately, while living at a blinding pace and burning the
proverbial candle at both ends as fast as I could, everyone who ever
got close to me got burned a bit. Like standing too close to a raging
bonfire. In some ways I am more than ready to die, having experienced
more than many people will ever even imagine in their lifetimes. I
literally did just about everything I ever wanted to do. Well, except
skydive. I missed that one unfortunately. The fact is I lived my life full
of zest, and danced with the best. In so many ways I was blessed, I
do mean blessed beyond belief or reasoning . . . go figure.

My greatest regret in life was that I was not a better father. You see you only get one chance to get it right, and I simply blew it. I was so busy, playing in bands, partying my ass off and raising hell that I missed my girls almost entirely. I had lots of money and spoiled them with material things and a private nanny and literally every extracurricular activity known, but I was never there to spend precious time with them, being a good dad when I had the chance to do so. I was too busy being a rock star at least in my own mind, and in the end lost the two people who mean the most to me. I love my daughters with all my heart and every fiber of my being. I just wish I had taken the time to be with them when I had the chance to be a Daddy. It is not surprising at all that they do not wish to take the time to be there for me now . . . go figure.

Anyway, my life could be summed up by the old cliché Sex-Drugs-Rock-N-Roll. Way too many drugs for real. As I said, in many ways I lived my life without regrets and full of adventure, but if I had the chance to do it all over again, I would live for my children instead. The thing is, none of us get a second chance . . . not really. Time passes us by and we have to live with the consequences of our actions, or in my case die for them.

So . . . when I die and I am on my way to Neverland and ever after, throw a party and certainly hope no one will cry for me. I am more than ready when the day comes, and yes, I have made my peace with the man upstairs . . . it's all good for real! I would rather those who know me throw a party and truly dance and sing to celebrate the good things my life represents, and there were so many good times for real. GOD and their guardian angels will take care of my girls in the end. He's been doing alright so far, and got them out of harm's way in time . . . THANK GOD! So . . . basically, don't cry for me, tomorrow's just another day!

"Passion" - Anthony Shore

"Hope" - Anthony Shore

Danielle Simpson
#999370

Age: 29
Education: Eleventh grade

Beyond the Shadow of a Doubt

At times, I sit wondering with some of the strangest things and ideas free styling through my mind. Though when your mind goes blank, that's it. It's more or less a major indifference to think and sustain a concrete focus. And so I speak, that it's beyond the shadow of a doubt that what's loaded in the clip of your mind will eventually be released in the chamber of your intentions. Especially, when the motivations and self determinations of your reactions touch the trigger of your actions. Likewise, I find myself quite often, so randomly striving through and beyond the shadows of a doubt when circumstances are being violated disgracefully. But in now-a-days timing, so it seems that everything is so essential and aggressive. So, I may say that to define this, arising from a spiritual point of view in 1 Corinthians 12:14, it states: "Now there are diversities of gifts, but the same spirit." So being that I am a conscious soul survivor. Yes indeed there are such times that I experience periods of isolation of being alone in this cold and interlude features of this evil world. But even then, I'm still willing to set aside my personal indifferences of life and grow. Because living in this lifetime really and truly wasn't meant for us to be. It was a set up, that's why it's such a struggle just to live and survive. Therefore, I ask the question: "How does one blend his or her cultural beliefs with spiritual discipline?" Because when the worst experiences of one's life are being reflected back upon that individual, then that alone may be the very thing that turns you to the deeper understanding of what's been missing or overlooked the most in your life.

So it's beyond the shadow of a doubt, that I often remain withstanding, lost in the closed caption of my thought. As if I was standing on the edge of a high cliff looking across the nature of my surroundings as the wind softly circulates a gentle breeze. But yet here again, back at one, wondering with a great sum of thoughts running in my mind like the waves in the ocean. Indeed shall I speak and say that I am the Alpha and Omega of mankind and thus more I am at one with my utmost Creator. In general aspects that I stand on a dignified principle. Likewise at brief, I would like to say this unto all before I enclose my maintenance of heartfelt inspirations. Though it's not easy living beyond the shadows of a doubt, nor is it easy living in the physical world and being tempted by physical lust. That of which you struggle to keep your mind focused on a higher consciousness of which you see no physical evidence. Therefore you must understand the metaphysical principles that dictate how and why such practices work. Otherwise, you'll only remain living "Beyond The Shadows Of A Doubt" struggling to survive "BEYOND THE SHADOW OF A DOUBT"!

If I Could Turn Back the Hands of Time

If I could turn back the hands of time, God knows I truly would, without a doubt. Thinking back to the good old days, it was hard but through it all, I managed to survive. And now seeking in the future to come, some better days. But does this episode of reality really exist? Because through the trials and tribulations of this lifetime, I've had many dark and lonely days and nights to come at once. I've been caught up in some of the worst of times and circumstances, that I honestly just couldn't see myself coming through nor enduring. So amidst of it all, it was somewhat beyond the visions of the enterprised revelations that there's a time of the day when the sun is truly indeed going down. And as it fulfills such actions, then that's when I begin my contemplating as is—"If I Could Turn Back The Hands of Time"? And though sometimes I often shed tears, I feel ashamed as though to say I'm only human as well. More so, I am the "Man's Child," "The Alpha and the Omega"!

So when it's my time to go before judgment day, yourself neither another will be able to answer the consequences of my life's calling. Only me, myself and I will be the attestation of my judgment day. But only if I just had the "one time" opportunity of going back and rewinding back the hands of time, that's embraced my life since birth, up until this point of my life span as of now, I would. And though I'm quite assured that many of you would agree the same. That is picture perfect! The revelation of your last and final day coming near to meet and salute you to your dying day and time. Would you embed yourself in fear? Honestly, what would you do? Cause the truth of the matter is this, you don't have to be imprisoned here where I am and be living on borrowed times as I am. Instead, if you are a living individual period, you're on death row yourself.

The only difference that upholds the form of indifferences is that, as I remain incarcerated (locked down in the system), amidst this prison society, a great mass majority of you all are amidst the liberations of the free world and out there death is discovered to be everywhere internationalized. But in this instance, I see death right around the corner! Whereas I speak, yes I would love to delight with my children and loved ones again because I've learnt that separations do bring out and about the utmost greatest of appreciations. And through the many lessons taught beyond the sufferings of me against all odds test of time. I only wish that . . . "If I could Turn Back The Hands of Time"!!!

Respectfully,
3rd EYE A*K*A
D. Simpson

Jack Smith
#000615

(Editor's note: Smith, at seventy-one, is the oldest man on death row and has served thirty-one years. He is called "Old Man.")

Age: *71*
Education: *Sixth grade*

I've been wrongfully incarcerated for thirty-plus years.

I will tell you what's on the transcript. My co-defendant was going to trial the same date and hour that I was, just in another courtroom. They saw that they did not have any evidence on me, because truth is, I wasn't a part of that crime in any way so they stopped his trial, and made him a deal for a life sentence as long as he'd testify to convict in my trial. The state's witnesses could not make identity on none of those people involved, besides that the shooter was six feet tall. Note: I am five feet, seven inches tall. Therefore, to try to make an ID for my trial, they took a picture of me to the state's witnesses a day before my trial date. Then the very day of my trial, DAs showed those same witnesses the same picture of me asking them for identification. Their witnesses said, "why yeah, that's the same picture you showed us at the 'house meeting' yesterday."

The only evidence they could present against me was my co-defendant saying I had the dead man's gun when, in fact, that gun was found in [name withheld]'s bedroom under his bed with his and the dead man's fingerprints on it (The Gun) "Not Mine." My car was stolen and used in the crime, then not properly dusted for prints to tell who stole it.

Life here for me has been a cruel and unusual punishment. Will you allow me to continue to face this punishment?

Richard Tabler
#999523

Age: 29
Hometown: Turlock, California
Last school: Turlock High School, Turlock, California
Education: Twelfth grade
Interests: Soccer, motocross, and cooking
Favorites: Book - the Bible; Movie - Boyz n the Hood; Ice cream - butter pecan; Motorcycle - CBR F-3
Other info: I'm very protective of my mom and sister and baby niece. I'm also a firm believer in taking responsibility for your actions.

Please try to keep an open mind while reading all that's below.

My full name is Richard Lee Tabler, better known by most as "Blue." The story I share with you is not about my crime or how I got here, but about how I caused a system lockdown in the state of Texas. I've been on Texas Death Row for two years. In those couple years, I've sat back and watched to see what officers would be "easy" targets along with inmates. It took me some time and being treated like an animal that I decided to do something about the way I was being treated as well as others. So I won't take all the credit for what was found in my cell.

On October 20, 2008 a cell phone was found in my cell on which I had been in direct contact with Senator John Whitmire. We had been calling each other's cell phones for over two weeks, talking about the treatment/confinement here on Death Row. Sometime during the second week, I told the senator I couldn't do something he asked me to do, which I guess didn't sit well with him. He reported I had a cell phone and had called and threatened him, which is a lie. So now after I showed the state of Texas they knew nothing about "High Tech Security" and that Death Row is a joke, the media and other organizations are reaching out to my fellow inmates on Death Row. Some people out there are talking about killing me, etc. Well my time will come soon enough, for on September 30, 2008 I dropped all my appeals and asked for an execution date, which I'll get by the middle of 2009.

    Sincerely,
    R. Tabler

Charles Thompson
#999306

Age: 38
Hometown: Tomball, Texas
Last school: Massy Business College, Houston; North Harris College, Tomball
Education: Eleventh grade/GED
Interests: Fishing, hunting, outdoor activities, water sports, skiing
Favorites: Author - Jeffrey Deaver; Movies - Shawshank Redemption, Indiana Jones movies, Star Wars; Ice cream - really like Blue Bell Mint Chocolate Chip, Moolenium Crunch, Banana Split; Car - Pantera De Tomaso
Other info: Family comes first. I'm a devout Catholic. My motto in life—the only dumb question is the one you don't ask! I believe in life's journey if you want it bad enough—nothing should stand in your way to make your dreams reality. I value morals, integrity, champions of causes, people with selfless compassion.

Greetings from the row.

What is life like on death row—a most commonly asked question of the death row prisoner. It is very much like the same day over and over. Similar to the movie *Groundhog Day*. After years it's become dull, you can have autopilot type days—you just go through.

Most days are spent reading. Music is a big part of our day—since Texas death row was moved to this super segregation facility unit we no longer have TVs. I think about my children, family, parents, grandparents every day. It's got to be the hardest on holidays, Christmas being the saddest time of year, a lonely time. It's a joyful time to celebrate Christ too. I often find myself thinking back to those fun filled x-mas mornings as a kid! The best memories of childhood. Who can forget those Christmas mornings!

The situation, circumstances that led to my being sent here

are compelling to say the least. Such medical causation issues, the confusing legal terms and definitions of concurrent causation—usually leads one to ask, how can two separate events or people be held responsible for one thing?

The system we have is not perfect by any means. I have a very colored opinion of the system—from both sides of the razor wire fences. As a former hard line Republican I used to think all criminals were guilty and got their just punishment.

After being flung into the system—to see how one sided it can be—I had my eyes opened to the real world. Long gone are the suburban misconceptions and sheltered views I once held. It is a faulty system we have. As with any thing—it's subject to error also.

The most special memories I hold dearest—the birth of my daughter and son, as I delivered them (with midwife assistance), childhood dreams, memories of playing as a kid—carefree times. Fishing, running around on a warm Texas summer night. Being in the beautiful mountains of Colorado.

Such sights as Pike's Peak, the Continental divide—mountain passes . . . to have been fortunate enough in life to have seen glaciers and national forest—our national parks and the ocean at sunset on the Texas coast.

I have a lot of fond memories—I think in life. It's the simple things we all take for granted—we never really appreciate them until we lose them. The most simple thing can trigger the memories of childhood.

For instance, in Texas prisons they mop the floor with Pine-o-pine. A similar cleaning solution to Pine-Sol. My mom used to get up on weekend mornings and clean house with Pine-Sol. I often get woke up here in prison by that pine smell—sometimes I lay there half awake and think I am at home . . . just as I'd get woke up growing up, by that pine smell.

For a moment I am not in prison, I am back home, and oh how sweet a feeling it is to hold for just that waking moment. Freedom comes in many forms. A brief dream, a distant memory . . . one can be physically incarcerated, but free in his mind—his thoughts—actions and how he chooses to look at life's journey.

I believe in the years ahead our country is going to go through many more changes. It's a turbulent time we live in now. To see the most diverse nation rise up and unite in the hardest of times is a testament of the very making of America. Land of opportunity, home of the free, land of the brave. My view is we are at a crossroads with this election. It's going to shape this country and determine our future in many ways. Our planet is going through such drastic changes, as well as the state of the world conflicts. It's a tumultuous event—War. I believe the people are more focused on peace, change, to focus on a better world. Call me a dreamer—but without dreams what is there? Hope—I am a prisoner of hope.

Retribution or Redemption

Retribution is just another word for revenge. Is it any surprise retribution is one of many arguments made for the support of capital punishment—as if death of a person is again balanced by the vengeful execution of another life. That fundamentalist view diminishes us all as a civilized society. All too often the pro-death penalty culture claim that retribution is self justifying, a simple payback. Some use the Holy Bible: (Exodus 21:23, 24) "You shall give life for life, eye for eye, tooth for tooth." Religious scholars actually teach that the eye for an eye scripture was an attempt to curtail violence in that period in early civilization (the Old Testament times), Biblical times in the Hebrew Culture, not in our millennium.

Any intelligent study of scripture must be viewed in the full context of the whole Bible. Indeed we as a society don't condone executing people for adultery. Conversely, it's glamorized daily in our culture, as idolatry. It's safe to worship false idols and go on living. We've advanced in many areas yet taken steps backwards with the use of politics and the death penalty. "As I live, says the Lord, I swear I take no pleasure in the death of the wicked man, but rather in the wicked man's conversion, that he may live" (Ezekiel 33:11). Understanding the Bible in its historical context, upon reading Ezekiel 33:11 you've read the Lord's swear. His wish is for man's redemption, not vengeful execution. Let's not overlook the sermon on the mount (Matthew 5:1-7:29) wherein Christ's focus is on mercy, reconciliation, and redemption. The forgiveness and passage into Heaven is available to all.

As Jesus himself was facing the death penalty, so were "two other men both criminals" were also led out with Jesus to be executed (Luke 23:39). One of the criminals who hung there hurled insults at him: "Aren't you the Christ—save yourself and us" (verse 40). But the other criminal rebuked him: "Don't you fear God" he said since you are under the same sentence (verse 41). We are all punished justly for getting what our deeds deserve. "But this man has done nothing wrong" (verse 42). Then he said "Jesus remember me when you come into your kingdom" (verse 43). Jesus answered him, "I tell you, the truth, today you will be with me in Paradise."

You've read it yourself folks, there was only one man in the whole Bible that Jesus ever personally promised a place with him in paradise. Not Peter, not Paul, not any of the disciples. He pardoned a convicted thief being executed with Jesus, on the cross next to him.

It should be offensive to the least faithful believer that the Bible justifies executing people. This message was brought to you by a condemned man, a believer in Christ's message and teachings. The power, truth, and teachings are all his and ours. My utmost to his highest.

In Christ,
Charles Thompson

Michael Toney
#999314

Editor's note: Toney put his execution up for sale on eBay in 2000.

Age: *43*
Education: *Tenth grade*

On October 8, 2008 the state (the Tarrant County DA) and my counsel asked the district court to overturn my conviction because of "prosecutorial misconduct." On October 12, the judge agreed and asked the Circuit Court of Appeals to overturn the conviction. My case is extraordinary as has been my life. I will leave death row in the next several weeks.

Michael's Story

Things are just not as simple as most people think and the rest have a tendency to over complicate the simple.

Is it possible with all of our state-of-the-art technology for someone to be convicted and sentenced to death without as much as a molecule—a scintilla—of evidence? If you don't believe it's possible and maybe even commonplace, you're probably expecting that jolly, bearded fellow wearing the red suit to slide down your chimney, too. Do you believe it is possible for someone to be convicted and sentenced to death row for a crime they have no personal knowledge of and didn't even hear about until twelve years after it occurred? What about a crime where there is no motive or connection to the victims? How about if the person has never been to the place the crime occurred; in fact, didn't even know such a place existed? Ideally, any one of these reasons should be enough to prevent a conviction/miscarriage of justice, shouldn't it? Maybe on television that's how it works, but not in the real world. Trials are not about the truth—they're "convicting contests." I know that's hard to swallow, but it's the truth.

In a trial the prosecution does everything possible to "convince" twelve people of something that may have no basis in reality. Twelve average people who almost certainly give a leg up to the state and probably don't really believe in or comprehend the "presumption of innocence." The state doesn't have to convince all of them of the same thing either. Some may believe one thing and the rest something altogether different, but as long as they all "think" the person is guilty that's all it takes. What are "fact" and "truth" in a jury trial? Common sense tells us that FACT is something that is indisputable. To any rational person there is only one TRUTH and that truth is the opposite of anything that is false. But in a jury trial the jurors hear the testimony and then decide what to believe and what not to believe. What they believe becomes FACT as a matter of law. Under our constitution and laws, a jury's decision is set in stone barring something extraordinary. Often newly discovered DNA evidence that excludes the convicted isn't enough to overturn the jury's decision. Even when the witnesses retract their testimony and admit it was a lie, the verdict often stands as TRUTH and FACT. We often hear the age old maxim: "The truth speaks for itself," but this is absurd. In a jury trial the truth is whatever the prosecution or defense convinces those twelve people of and usually the one with the most resources is the most convincing.

The United States Supreme Court opinioned: "it is Constitutional to execute the innocent as long as they have had a fair trial." That defies logic, doesn't it? I'm telling you now that any innocent person convicted has not had a fair trial, but proving the unfairness is a whole different matter. Even if it is proven, it's still indescribably difficult to overcome those twelve ordinary, fallible people's truth-detecting abilities and final decision or verdict.

Before I move on I want to apologize for my rough and abrupt transition from subject to subject. After more than eleven years of the misery of injustice and constantly fluctuating between hope and despair, that is precisely how my mind works. Nothing is more unreasonable than injustice. I am intimate with the misery of injustice.

My personal injustice began on December 4, 1997. I was accused of a horrible crime that was committed twelve years earlier. On the evening of Thanksgiving 1985, [several people] went to a convenience store for some snacks. When they returned they found a briefcase allegedly on the porch of their home. They took it inside and opened it. It exploded, instantly killing three of them, except for one woman, who was sleeping in another room, and her son. The crime was the longest running investigation in the history of the Bureau of Alcohol, Tobacco, and Firearms (BATF). The BATF is synonymous with the murder of Randy Weaver's family at Ruby Ridge and the incineration of the Branch Davidian men, women, and children in Waco, Texas. They also wrongfully accused Richard Jewell of the Olympic Bombing in Atlanta.

During the twelve-year investigation, countless theories and suspects were considered. Then in 1996, after the Oklahoma City Murrah Federal Building bombing, the BATF reopened or jumpstarted unsolved domestic bombing, which is a rare crime in this country. The BATF intended to close the books on the unsolved domestic bombings, by any means. It was about this same time that I became reacquainted with [name withheld], when I first met him in 1989. During the course of our casual conversation, he informed me that he had recently been given a polygraph test concerning a bombing that killed an entire family in Lake Worth, Texas. He told me: "They think I dropped off my friend, and that he placed the briefcase bomb." He didn't tell me who was killed, when it happened or why. I assumed, which is never a good thing, that the crime was recent.

A few weeks later, I met another man. He had recently been arrested in Azle, Texas for possession of an explosive component. When he told me, the first thing I thought is: "Azle borders Lake Worth," which brought what the other man had told me to mind. At first, I thought the explosive component of what he told me was somehow connected. A reasonable deduction considering the proximity of Lake Worth to Azle, the unusual nature of the crime (bombing) and the fact that the men told me about "bombing and bomb components" just weeks apart. After some discussion about what he was actually arrested for, I told him about what the other man had told me. He knew more about the Lake Worth bombing than I did, but he wasn't certain when it happened or who was killed either. He had heard something about the wrong people being targeted. That was the extent of our communal knowledge of the bombing and what was hearsay upon hearsay.

To make a long story somewhat shorter, the one man, in order to bargain himself out of a bind, told the authorities I confessed to him. My name was never mentioned in the investigation until that man lied to the investigators.

When the newly-formed task force began looking into the story, they were in the process of presenting evidence to a grand jury on another man. The first person the BATF interviewed concerning me was my ex-wife, my very biased ex-wife, who I hadn't seen since October 1989. They didn't ask her about the crime though. They had long ago given up on casual inquiries. They told her they knew I had committed the crime and showed her the very gruesome crime scene photos, which had become standard operating procedure for the desperate task force. She responded with the most truthful statement made: "Michael, kill someone in a bombing, you're nuts." She didn't know anything about any bombing. However, because they told her they 'knew' (a lie) that I was responsible and because of the horrific crime scene photographs, her natural curiosity was peaked. She went and asked her parents what they heard about a bombing in Lake Worth and then "ran to the library." She researched the old news stories.

The next day she allegedly called the BATF back and said something about being in that area with me and my ex-business partner, fishing on the night of Thanksgiving 1985. This is not a lie on her part. It is just a mistake and confabulation based on the agents telling her they "knew." She told them that we went to the lake, that it was a "chilly" night and that my ex-business partner and I had .22 caliber rifles and that I shot a beaver. She also said that we traveled to the lake in our 1979 Chevrolet Silverado pickup truck and that the rifles were on a rack in the truck. All of this is true, except the night we actually went to the lake. We didn't go to the lake or anywhere together on the night of Thanksgiving. It was the coldest day of the year up to that point. It was below freezing, not "chilly!" Records prove that the two rifles were purchased by my ex-business partner on December 18 and 19, 1985 (an indisputable fact that he repeatedly denied) and I know that I didn't buy that truck until Friday, December 13, 1985. I recall the date of purchase vividly, because that truck ended up being "very bad luck."

It is impossible to go to the lake in a truck that was not yet in my possession and to shoot a beaver with a rifle that had yet to be purchased. Also, it was too damned cold to be "hanging out at the lake" like she said. But like I said and records prove, they had convinced her it had to be Thanksgiving, so the rest of the coercion/manipulation was easy for them. She gave a statement on October 7 and then started spending entire days with the BATF agents. They forced the confabulation/evolution of her statement to fit what they needed. Finally, late on the third day, they brought in a "cognitive interview" specialist from Washington. He succeeded at getting one word into her mind and out of her mouth again and that word was "briefcase." Then she described the briefcase I had used from 1987 to 1989. The description in no way fits the one that crime scene debris proved contained the bomb. She just confabulated everything with the help of the investigators. My wife had not heard of the bombing, my ex-business partner had not heard of the bombing, just as I hadn't heard about it until 1997. Nearly twelve years after the fact!

Breaking News! Breaking News! Breaking News!

It is the evening of Thursday, December 18, 2008. Another prisoner just sent me a note in which he wrote:

"I heard on the radio yesterday that the Court of Criminal Appeals agreed with the trial judge and overturned your case!!!"

As I wrote at the beginning of this (several days ago): "In the very near future I will leave death row." Of course, I am pleased with the "order overturning the wrongful conviction and returning my presumption of innocence," but I'm not surprised. The State (Tarrant County District Attorney's Office) in agreement with my counsel had admitted (only after being caught) to violating my right to a fair trial by withholding at least fourteen individual exculpatory records. The only reason they acknowledged the misconduct is they got caught, to give the false impression of doing what's right, and to avoid further scrutiny.

Christmas Eve 2008

It's too stressful, depressing, unreasonable, anxiety inducing to write this all in one session, so I'm doing it once a period of days and weeks.

Here it is Christmas Eve, the second loneliest, most depressing day of the year in this place of misery—second only to tomorrow. This revelation probably comes as a surprise to most as it would seem an individual's execution day would be the worst. But this is one of the most common misconceptions concerning death row and the condemned! Being on death row is not living. It is merely existing in a miserable environment. Death is the one certain thing that will end this misery. The execution ends the punishment!

I have stated since day one of this seemingly perpetual nightmare. They're either going to correct the injustice and send me home on my feet or turn the miscarriage of justice into a grave miscarriage of justice and send me home in a box. Contemplating my own death at the hands of the state has been comforting in that if truth proves too elusive and justice too expensive, it is a certain means to end the misery of injustice. Give me justice, something I believe every human being has an inalienable right to or send me before the Throne of the True Judge. He knows I am innocent. He doesn't have to rely on guessing games and speculation. He doesn't have to be convinced of anything by perverters of justice like [name withheld]. He knows I am innocent and knows my heart and will judge and reward me accordingly.

So, in a way, the court's order is disconcerting. The certain means to end the extraordinary pain, the humiliation, the utter misery of injustice has been removed. But like one of my lawyers told the media: "This is a big step in proving Michael's innocence." I agree it is, but isn't proving one's innocence contrary to the very fundamentals of our justice system? A person is supposed to be proven guilty by the prosecution! He's not supposed to have to prove his innocence! But in reality (the real world), any person on trial better be prepared to prove innocence. The inalienable fact is our system is designed to convict the guilty, not find the innocent, innocent! The supposed safeguards are just words that carry no weight, much like the "presumption of innocence." I may not have known or believed those things when this hellish ordeal began, but I know now.

Because of the court's decision—overturning the wrongful conviction and returning my presumption of innocence—I cannot continue this writing. I must now focus all of my energy on the potential trial and preventing another wrongful conviction.

Michael Toney
"An Innocent Man"

Carlos Trevino
#999235

Age: *33*
Hometown: *San Antonio, Texas*
Last school: *San Antonio High, San Antonio, Texas*
Education: *Ninth grade*
Interests: *Keeping kids from entering prison, learning about animals*
Favorites: *Authors - Nicholas Sparks, Danielle Steele*

<u>Who are We?</u>

Who are we? I am not just talking about those of us in here. But I am talking about you and I, those around us. Many of y'all will know who you are. Many don't know who they are. Others just don't care . . . In everything that I write is by experience and where life has taken me. So who are we in general? We use everyone around us, our family, children and friends as if their trust and love were expendable and meaningless. We think of ourselves first and others second. "We lie, cheat and steal in little ways, thinking it's unimportant, justifying it by saying to ourselves that others do it, so it is okay that we do it too. We almost trust no one. We have no understanding nor patience with the wrongs and mistakes of others (BUT WE WANT ALL THE WRONGS AND MISTAKES). We have no empathy for their despair; we have no compassion for their suffering and misery. The lost souls that roam the streets are not our concern; they are examples of our failure and our embarrassment to us. It's best to ignore them. If they have nowhere to live it's their own fault. If they happen to disappear, it will provide us with space to live and breathe, for they cause nothing but trouble."

People all around us are fast to complain about prostitution, gang and criminal activity. Always expecting for the police or those in authority to fix the problem(s). Always expecting someone else to fix the problem(s), when they themselves can try to fix the problem(s). Or try to reach out to those lost souls. Especially children or a child.

Most of us become lost souls as children. For many different reasons. When a child steps into the streets, within the first breath they inhale, they lose their innocence. By the time they exhale, they are now twice as old.

Many of us (you and I) know of a lost soul or child who is turning down the wrong road. But do we try to reach out to that lost soul or child? No, we complain, call the police and blame everyone else, starting with that lost soul or child parent(s). We are fast to judge that lost soul or child, never knowing their story. Instead, we are fast to hate this lost soul, because they have on ragged clothes. What makes that child or lost soul (or poor people) so different? Are we really not worth the air we breathe?

So, when these people who are fast to complain and judge, as soon as they see this lost soul or child do something wrong, they are fast to YELL for justice and for BLOOD. It's easy to wish my death simply because I am on death row. It's easy to read about me and judge me without knowing my story nor the law or the truth. If it's death that you wish for me, that is okay. But let me ask you this . . . how will my death solve anything? Will my death prevent the possibility of lost souls taking innocent lives? What will my death teach these lost souls and people? Will murders stop? To really judge a lost soul on a personal level is a lot harder because you have to get to know the person. So it's easier to judge, hate and wish me dead. 'Cause as humans we are faster to hate and kill. But we are extremely slower to try to love and heal each other. To hate and kill takes no skills. But to love and heal, takes skills.

My point is that the next time you see a lost soul or child, try reaching out to them. ' Cause tomorrow's wrongs and mistakes will be done by our children. So, if we can reach a child or lost soul and show them the right path of life, then chances are that we will not only save one life, but the lives of innocent people in the future. I know that we can't save all the lost souls. But when one lost soul is saved, so is the possibility of innocent lives.

If you don't wish to reach out to a lost soul or child, then don't be so fast to judge, hate, kill and yell for justice or BLOOD when that lost soul does something wrong, especially when you had the chance to reach out to that lost soul.

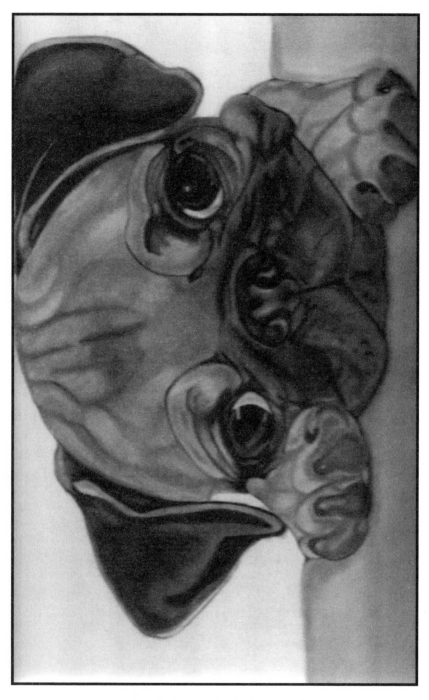

"Take Me Home" - Carlos Trevino

Who I Am

Where did life start for me? As I sit on death row, I have thought about this over and over. I believe it's fair to say life started out hard for me and my family. Our status never changed, and I question that a lot. At first I didn't think a blind person could change or that you could change a blind person. People who are blind can change. For most they do not learn until it's too late.

I am the oldest child of my family. Then comes my brother, who is also in prison. Then comes my sister. When I was born it was only my mother and I. My mother married this guy, sad to say, he was my father. My father walked out of our lives before I was born. What was the reason? I don't know and I have never asked my mother. I just know that I grew up without a father.

As far back as I could remember we were always on the streets. When my father left, my mother struggled. She was just seventeen years old and never finished school. Family members would turn her away when she asked for help. I don't know why and I never really asked. After some time my mother met a man. He pretty much took care of us and soon we had a place to live. At first all was beautiful, but as always the devil comes out and shows his ugly face, planting his seeds of pain, sadness and hate with the love for destruction. By this time my brother was born. My mother wasn't a nice lady and she wasn't a small lady. When she would get mad, she would beat up my brother and me. Since I was the oldest, I always got the worst of it! She would hit me with anything and everything. She would beat me up as if I were nothing more than an unwanted dog. I can remember beatings when I was five years old. To this day, I have always wondered why my mother would beat me so. I never really asked her.

I believe that I was around eight years old when the seeds were starting to grow out of my heart. I was beginning to hate my mother. I never realized that till I landed in jail in 1993 when I was eighteen years old. I hated the way my mother would beat up my brother and me. I hated it 'cause I was just a helpless child. I also wonder if she realized that. My mother and her man would love to go out drinking and partying all night. Since we were kids they couldn't always leave us at home by ourselves, so they took us to bars. Sometimes we would go in and other times we would stay outside in the car. Of course most of the time we would stay at home by ourselves. At this time I was around eight years old and my brother was six. Being children many times we would end up at our neighbor's house. 'Cause when

"Brothers" - Carlos Trevino

night came, everything looked so scary! We were scared and ran to our neighbor's house and of course they would take us in. But that came with a price. My mother always told us to stay in the house. When my mother came home and didn't find us at home, she knew exactly where to find us. She would pick us up and when we got home we would get a beat down for not staying home.

My mother had a love for going out by herself. She would leave and be gone for days, leaving us kids with her boyfriend. Her boyfriend would go crazy and mad. So, like a madman he would look for my mother everywhere and he would take us with him. I can remember one time when her boyfriend spotted my mother in a car. It was late at night and we were in a truck. My brother and I were asleep in the back. He started chasing my mother all over the street. My brother and I were rolling all over in the back of the truck trying to hang on to something. Luckily the truck had a camper.

When he would catch my mother, he would beat her extremely bad. Watching this with my own eyes would really scare me to death. How could a person lose so much blood and turn so many colors and still live? I was an eight year old child and I was scared to death. Many times as my mother lay on the floor with her eyes swollen shut and busted lips and blood all around her, I honestly thought she wouldn't get up.

She did get up. She would just clean up the mess and pretend nothing happened and protect her boyfriend when people would see and ask about what happened. I hated that man for beating my mother, and so another branch of hate grew out of my heart. I lost count as to how many times this happened. One night he started hitting my mother and she ended up calling the cops. They took him away and my mother ended the relationship. She packed what she could and we were on the street again. My sister was already born by then. My siblings have different fathers. I don't think I was nine yet when all of this had taken place.

We stayed with relatives and a lot of times I could see it in their eyes they really didn't want us to stay with them. I could see the hate in their eyes, and so another branch of hate grew from my heart. We moved a lot because one knows when they are not welcome. We also moved a lot because we had no money, only what the government provides, which in Texas isn't much. So, we moved from one bad neighborhood to another. From one housing project to another. Finally we settled down in the projects, but during all of this not much changed. My brother and I were left alone at home. My mother left

"Curious" - Carlos Trevino

with my sister and took her everywhere. Every once in a while she stayed with us. My brother and I pretty much did what we wanted. At a very young age we learned to handle our disagreements and problems with violence, especially against each other.

Life really kicked off for me around the age of eleven. I was already smoking marijuana. Being in the streets, by the age of twelve I was already sexually active, and getting into more and more trouble. At thirteen, I was arrested for the first time and it never ended. I think around the age of fourteen, my mother saw there was no changing me. But it was through her and the man she was with that I learned of violence. My mother loved fighting and she fought like a man. She was always beating up other women and she loved it. It was also through her and her friends that I learned about drugs. As my mother looked at me and tried to tell me about not getting into so much trouble, I believe that she saw it in my eyes there was no changing me. She could tell me not to do something, yet I would still do it. I will never forget the words she told me that day.

She told me, "If I knew you were gonna turn out this way, I would have never sold myself for you when you were a baby." I guess she would have let me die. She was telling me that I wasn't worth anything, that I was a nobody. So my life jumped to a life of destruction. Those words never left my mind or heart. I was a child who didn't know any better nor was I too bright.

I never knew how much I hated and loved my mother until Thanksgiving 1992. My mother tried to hit my brother and of course we were all drinking and partying. But when I saw that, I lost it. Things got very ugly, but watching my mother trying to hit my brother . . . all the years of abuse came rushing out of me. I had bottled it all up inside. I wasn't that helpless child anymore.

That day I whispered in my mother's ear, for her to never hit my brother again. I knew my mother was scared of me. She had stopped hitting me when I turned twelve. I had become this young man with no conscience. Everything that I had been through made me this person. The violence that I was so scared of as a young child was now just a way of life. I hate that part of my life. I wish that I had become a better person when my mother told me those words, but I only got worse.

My life started in a broken home where violence was the answer. A home where hate grew. Where pain and hurt come before LOVE. Where I thought I was a real man. But I was only an emotionally unbalanced child with no guidance nor understanding of what love or life was and what a real family should be. Of course my life nor story ends here. This is just what my broken home was like.

Now let me tell you what the streets were like and how most of my fellow prisoners and friends minds were formed.

Broken Social Skills

I can sit here and tell you the stories of many many many lost souls and how they (we) end up in prison or even death row. Throughout my time of being in prison, and on death row, most of the stories I hear are just about the same. On a rare occasion I find someone who had everything and yet still ended up in here. And so it's easy to fall into this place. But most of us in here never had that chance at life.

Growing up, most of us grew up in bad neighborhoods, ghettos, projects, government housing or whatever you wish to call them. Where most people wouldn't step into, unless they lived there. Unfortunately most of us here had nowhere else to go. And stepping out of our hoods wasn't sunshine either. For people were fast to let you know you didn't belong outside of your hood. You would get funny stares and pointing fingers at you, whispering something about you. Or simply given a look of pure hate. I hated going places with my mother when I was a child. I could always feel those stares from people. But it was those same stares that planted another seed of hate in my heart. Lord only knew how fast that would grow. Even as you read this, it's happening to some child out there.

It all begins at home. Most of us come from broken families. Where most of the time there is only one parent, the mother. Which is very hard for her. She probably works, comes home, cooks, cleans, washes clothes and by the time she knows it it's the following day. Being a single parent of one child. And being this busy so you can't keep your eyes on your child at all times, much less when there is more than one child. And so because life demands money, a parent or parents are hardly at home. Then we come from families that are abusive mentally, physically, and sexually. These abuses happen on a daily basis. Then you have parent(s) with drug addictions. As children we live through this. It becomes a way of life. We start off emotionally unbalanced. We hide and never speak of things going on in our homes. But if a person would only see with a heart, the signs would be everywhere. Instead those stares of hate bring out another leaf of hate within the heart.

As we turn to the streets, we meet other children just like us in our hoods. These children become our new family, they fill in the void we carry in our hearts. The love we don't get at home. And so a street gang begins, if it has not already formed. That comes with a price. We are instantly introduced to drugs, if we aren't already doing them since we learn it from home. In these drugs we find an answer to our problems. To forget what really happens around us. But as children we don't have a clue that drugs are only a temporary solution. And so a greater problem begins, "addiction." What began as something cool or as a solution ends up controlling your life. In one form or another.

Violence is started almost as soon as we learn to walk. Violence is our daily bread. I can't remember ever being in the hood, at someone's house and someone was not fighting. As children we were taught, as most Americans, that if someone hits you, you hit them back. As children we fight with our brothers and sisters, with our neighbors etc. Violence would start instantly when a child is emotionally unbalanced. We find violence is the answer to life. Never realizing that at home we are taught to handle our problems with violence. Almost immediately when we hang around with other children, violence starts. One, we fight to prove ourselves to our new family. (That's the price.) And it's a cycle. Those older kids were put through the same test. Today, tomorrow, next month, next year, the younger children will be put through the same test. The blind lead the blind.

At some point other children from different hoods come and beat us up. Sometimes we are stabbed, sometimes shot. And many times children don't make it to see another sunrise. When any of this happens, the following day, weeks, months or even years, more children are hurt or killed for retaliation never falls short and many times the price is very high. We never stop to think that all we do is hurt and kill each other. We defend and protect our hoods, territories when we own nothing in them. We never stop and realize that those kids in the other hoods are just like us. We only destroy what little we have. And we never build anything positive. Nothing!

While all of this is happening we steal and rob violently, to get drugs. We sell drugs to stay high, make ends meet or for weapons for our new family. Everyday we wake up to this environment as children we are taught these social skills. So life itself becomes a way of survival. It becomes a survival like the wild. The animals prey on each other. The young animals are taught right away of predators. The young animals grow up learning how to survive. And all it knows is what it's taught, survival. It's the way of the wild. If you were to see a young bear caught in a bear trap, and you were trying to help this bear. When you got near this bear, chances are it will try to get away from you. Or the bear will attack you. The bear is using his survival instincts. And it doesn't know any better that you're trying to help it. And so as children we adapt to our environment. The social skills we learn around become our survival.

Many times our parent(s) at home grew up in the same environment. Their parent(s) grew up in the same hood. So they don't know any better. So, it is okay for their kid of twelve, thirteen, fourteen, fifteen years old to have a girlfriend or boyfriend. It is okay for them to have sex. It is okay for them to act violently. It is okay for them to do drugs. For them to be in and out of juvenile facilities.

This is just a summary as to where many of us come from, not all, but most of us. All you have to do is open a newspaper or watch the news. And you'll see that the cycle continues. In the hood we are made to believe that this is the only way of life. Which is a lie. For some of us we learn a little too late. Some of us die before seeing our twenty-first birthday. Some of us end up in prison for the rest of our lives. The rest of us wait to be executed. How does one break the cycle? How does one change a lost soul, or how does one change? I am not sure, but one thing I know for sure, there is nothing in prison for no one! And only death awaits you on death row. Anyone living this life. It's never too late to change. Don't wait till it's too late. Get help any way you can. Make a change.

Love and blessings,
Carlos Trevino

Willie Trottie
#999085

Age: 39
Hometown: Houston, Texas and Alexandria, Louisiana
Last school: Bolton High School, Peabody Extension Campus
Education: Ninth grade
Interests: Government, politics, science
Favorites: Books - autobiographies, Clive Cussler; Ice cream - strawberry and butter pecan; Cars - GM cars, Mercedes

I'd consider myself a conservative Democrat. I'm a Christian. I do think Capital Punishment is okay in only certain cases—when it's applied appropriately and not discriminatory as it is now. I'm a Virgo and most character traits under this sign fit my personality, too. Thanks for wanting to know who's who on D/row. The "real" people we are, not what media or state agents have portrayed myself to be. Just ordinary people who made a terrible mistake in their lives, and now have to pay for this with their (our) life. Some, not all.

October 23, 2008. Thursday, 12:56 p.m.

I've tried to offer you an inside view from this side of the walls that separate death row men from free society. I must admit this is a rather hard emotional thing for me to do. Though, at the same time helpful, because it allows me to release my emotions in a way that helps me to cope and forgive myself for the situation that led me here. I'd hope that those who read this will not judge but only see, and feel where I am coming from or have tried to present myself.

I'm not sure if you are aware, though I would suspect that you are, that the prison system is on state-wide lock down, and due to this, it is somewhat hard for me to fully concentrate. D/row was on lockdown back on October 13. And, we thought it was the annual lockdown where contraband is searched for. It wasn't until a week later that we would learn the true cause of this lockdown.

Nevertheless, I tried to give you what you requested. It was sorta hard when you're cold and basically hungry from the lack of nutritional sack meals.

I am sympathetic for the experience that Senator Whitmire had to endure. However, I can say that, after years of being here and seeing how things manifest and propaganda is presented, I can see it was strategically done right before the holidays. Cell phones have been on death row for more than a year! Men on the row were caught with them. All the blame is not on the guards. This also could be contributed to the "access" that death row has to the general population inmates who come back here to d/row's building to work and too, those Administrative Segregation inmates who are also housed in 12-Building with d/row! So I think it's unfair to place all the blame on the guards. It is still a "security" breach regardless. But the whole picture is not presented to the public . . . like everything else, right?

What Life is Like on Death Row

What was life like on death row at Ellis One unit? When I first arrived at d/row back on December 16, 1993, I really didn't know what to expect. I was a first time inmate in the prison system. I remember limping down the long hallway, because I was still on crutches from the incident that led me to death row. I was recovering from multiple gunshot wounds. I remember limping with two guards escorting me to the infirmary for a check-up. Then from there we proceeded to the captain's office where I was asked some questions about the crime, my version of the crime, and taking photos of any tattoos or scars—markings to identify me in case of escape or death. I was given the run-down of what's expected of me, the general rules, and where I would be housed. Being that I was a non-problem inmate, my travel card followed me from the county jail. I was placed on a wing that was for docile, non-problem inmates. G-13 Wing, 1-row, 16 cell.

I remember walking into the wing, and seeing three tiers, where there were TVs attached to the walls on stands to my left as I walked down the runway, and on my right side were the cells the inmates were housed in.

When we walked to the wing the picket officer asked, "What cell?"

"16-cell," the guard called out.

As I limped my way down to the end, there were men standing at their doors; the cells were "open bars," regular prison bars. They could reach out and touch me if I walked closer to the bars. But I was in the middle of the two guards as they escorted me. I'd learn this was the escorting procedure; they used their bodies to protect you as a shield. As we walked what seemed like ages, we finally came to a small enclosed cell that was tight! There's twenty-one cells on each row, with three rows. As I walked by the cells, the men were standing there with large headphones on their heads. I would find out what they were used for. They were for the TV sound and the radio that was affixed to the wall. I'd be brought a pair later that evening.

It was about afternoon time when I arrived to d/row on a chilly December afternoon. After the door closed behind me, I sat on the small bunk with a mattress and pillow, cold, confused, and not knowing what to expect. I WAS not scared! I've been through much worse. I fought for my life to survive multiple surgeries and the gunshots. After what seems like hours had passed, I heard a thudding sound on my wall. It's my neighbor asking me my name: "What they call you? What you go by?" he asked. I told him "T-Rock." This is my nickname from the free world, not a prison made-up name like most guys do when they come to prison. He asked me if I needed anything. First defense is to say no! I'd learn later that is how d/row operates. New houses, new arrivals, come to d/row and they are given the basic necessities to hold them over until they are able to buy these items for themselves. At Ellis it didn't take that long. The commissary officer would allow you to buy things and deduct this from your account when it's cleared on the trust fund. Each offender arrives with a check cut from the county jail of his account that is deposited into his prison account, which could take days or weeks.

So for a couple of days, I didn't go to the shower, but bird bathed inside my small cage. I had no shower slides to wear to shower. You never shower with bare feet, you will get a serious infection, athlete's feet! No matter how much the showers are cleaned. It's cold down in this cell because I'd learn I'm right in front of the outside flex yard for the single man cages. Next to this was the much larger size recreation yard where up to fifteen or more men are recreated together. I'd learn some days later, after I'd been cleared by classification that I could be in group recreation. I'd be asked if I wanted to recreate? I said yes!

"Galatians" - Jose Rivera

But I was told that I could not have my crutches inside the dayroom or recreation yard, since they could be used as a weapon by me or against myself. I still went to recreation. I had to leave the crutches at the door, and hop to a nearby table and sit there for the three hours we were allowed recreation.

I'd introduce myself to the other guys and we played dominoes, chess, checkers, word scrabble, or watch TV. Others would be outside playing basketball or just walking up/down the large yard. It was funny to me how I'd entered the dayroom. I'd be strip searched and only allowed to wear my boxers and tennis shoes to the dayroom. Any clothes, back then, were the two piece, shirt, pants, or gym shorts. They would be carried by the officers. Being that I was on crutches, I was not handcuffed as most inmates were before exiting their cell. But I'd hop to the dayroom, the door would be open, where other inmates stood around or near the door and they could easily rush the guard opening the door, or another inmate who will be placed inside after the door is closed is still handcuffed. He's at the mercy of other offenders.

I'd hear tales of inmates being attacked as they walked into the dayroom handcuffed behind their backs, whilst the other inmates he'd gotten into it with earlier or days before were awaiting him and would attack. The guards would immediately close the door, and you're on your own. It wasn't until years later and after countless attacks on inmates, when it happened to a female guard who was no more than about four feet tall. She was rushed and bruised up pretty badly. Then, they installed a small cage within the dayroom that protected inmates and guards from attack by other inmates when the door was opened to let another inmate in. I noticed this first off, after doing security myself for some years. But as the Texas Department of Criminal Justice is known for, they only react after the action has occurred.

I'd eventually regain some strength back to my right leg and foot, the feeling and nerves would come back to life, and I could feel it which allowed me to interact with the guys and play basketball. I'd hop, stand back against the wall and shoot the ball, and then lean on the wall to wait for the ball to be passed to me, and I'd shoot again. I quickly got the hang of things there and pretty much adjusted in no time. I'd have my account (trust fund) deposited with cash which allowed me to make store (commissary). I'd now purchase more underclothing. I'd given most of it away in the county jail the day we were transferred to d/row. I say we, because I'd been transported with another condemned man. He'd years later be executed in November of 2006; in fact, it would be on the exact date that my trial had begun, November 8. There were about seven or more of us all tried for capital murder and we were all going to trial about the same time. Trials are mostly held during "election" time, to get a higher rate of convictions I'd later learn. So we had given our possessions away to a couple of guys who were back on bench warrant for a new trial. They too had been on d/row for ten years or more and they told us what we'd be allowed to take back with us and not. We'd soon learn after arriving to d/row that we were misled! We could have brought back all that we purchased in the county jail, from coffee pot, to underclothes, to food items. It was our first test and failure of believing inmates.

I quickly bought these things again because wearing boxer shorts or socks that someone else has worn is not my style. I hated when my brother would wear my socks. I bought the things that are essential, shaving mirror, soap, shower slides, hot pot, drinking cup, bowl, etc. and then other goodies, sweets, and boxers and socks to bundle up in because it was cold! After about a week, I'd get my first visit from my mother and son. I didn't have to call them and tell them we were leaving. They tell you early you're on the chain bus! This means you're headed to the big house, prison, for us, death row! I'd be placed inside a small cage to visit my family. It was something strange for my son to see me inside this cage, and being handcuffed, or uncuffed. He was only two years old at the time but knew something wasn't right. In the county when they'd visit, I was just behind a glass to him, but there was something different and it showed on his face that he didn't like it. I didn't want him to see this often because my mom would try to come every week. She only lived about half an hour from the prison in Houston, and Ellis One unit is right off I-45 North, a straight shot. Plus I didn't like her on the highways by herself, but Mom would still come, bless her soul. I lost her September 18, 2007, ten days after my thirty-eighth birthday. But the mother she'd become, she wanted to make sure I was okay, healing well from my wounds and surgery.

Some months would pass, and I'd hear (learn) about a "work capable" program for death row! I've always worked in my life, in fact, I was working three jobs at the time of this crime. So, I wanted to work! Didn't matter what it would be. I wanted to get out of this small cell. I'd hear that guys who worked could walk and prepare their own trays from a steam table, similar to buffet style and they would have cell mates. This was a turn off for some. They didn't want to work, nor share a cell with a stranger. But the cells were much larger. Plus, you'd be outside your cell all day long! Work consisted of a couple of jobs for death row—the Garment Factory, where the men would make and prepare the prison guard pants. The women would prepare the shirts. They didn't want both pants and shirts on the same unit, where an inmate could get it and try to escape.

I was first assigned to the garment factory where I'd sew the pockets. It was fun and there were various machines in this huge shop. Machines I'd seen before and some I knew how to operate and some I didn't. I learned to operate every machine out there! And often volunteered to work a guy's machine or shift if he had a lay in, special visit, or was on medical leave. There were many other men out in the factory too, along with guards who wore free world clothes, shop workers, though more inmates than them. Men had all sorts of tools in their possession, from twelve-inch long scissors, to screw drivers, various picks, that they would need to remove broken thread from the machines they used. All types of "weapons," I'd say to myself, and they said we're a FUTURE DANGER???!

I'd eventually relocate inside the building where I worked as a barber! I was the death row barber, where I could cut the inmates' hair who were on the work program, as well as those who didn't volunteer to work, where I'd first arrived on the row. I immediately enjoyed this job because I was responsible for making the guys look their best for visits with their family and friends who would come from all parts of the world to visit them. Unfortunately too, I'd also be their "pre-undertaker"! I didn't take too kindly to this job at first, but then I'd get some special requests where guys who really liked my haircuts would ask me to "fix 'em up" so they would look nice in their caskets for their families! This did come to me as a shock, and I never really thought of a job like that, but then, after consideration, I'd comply and then really took pride in what I did for the guys. Then I'd also work as SSI, this is like janitorial work. We'd be responsible for keeping the wing we lived on clean, dayrooms mopped, swept, and basically taking care of grown men who would throw trash everywhere.

Also, I'd be responsible for setting up the steam table, which meant placing water in the five slots about an hour before the food would be carted down from the main kitchen. Once there, I'd remove the larger pans of food and place them in the steaming water to be heated and set up other non-hot dishes on another stainless steel table next to this steam table and when chow was served, either lunch, dinner, or breakfast, they'd then roll the doors for the inmates on that particular row to come down and pick up a tray and serve themselves. The officer was only responsible for serving the main course, which would be the meat. However, most officers said, you're all grown men, serve yourselves, and don't cheat the next man behind you. It pretty much went smoothly. Occasionally there would be a knucklehead who would try the guard and get one more piece of meat, whether it was chicken or fish patty. After that row had been served, those men could either return to their cells and eat or eat inside the dayroom. Most would eat in the dayroom because after everyone was served, you were then allowed to go back through the line for extras (at the officer's discretion. Most of the time this was allowed, but there were always a few who would not. Other workers would give their helpings, too! I worked this job a few years, even trimmed some guard's heads, though this was forbidden. But if they told me to edge them up, I'd comply with their commands.

Basically I worked on this volunteer work program from summer 1994 until March 2000! There were some serious incidents that took place on d/row that would eventually shut it down. There were attempted escapes before I arrived on d/row whilst I was there which all occurred (not on work program) but in the Administrative Segregation areas. All would be from the flex yards, and one time was from the single man yard, another was from the group man yard. It wasn't until the escape of November 25, 1998, Thanksgiving escape that would end the d/row program! However, reports would later confirm that death row was indeed outgrowing its capacity there at the older prison, and we were relocated to another more modern facility. But all along there was a much grander scheme awaiting us. Remember the "future dangerous" comment? Well after many years, guys who worked with weapons, and with guards who were great-great grandmothers, grandfathers, kids straight from high school, women about four-feet tall and shorter—there was a cry from them for years saying that they had not harmed any one of these vulnerable guards or other inmates. These pleas went unanswered; however, they were acknowledged.

Then along came Ms. Karla Faye Tucker! She, with her pleas of a changed woman, new creation, Christian, which I don't doubt. But her cries were heard around the world! Men had been saying this for years and had many officers backing them saying they should be commuted in sentence, but they still face execution. Well, from Karla Faye's pretty face and cries about living on d/row for years and was no longer a threat, the prison officials were planning way before then, that things had to be changed! It was in essence "contradictive" to what the state DAs who sentenced, well the juries, had so said. Does the name of Johnny Paul Penry [a mentally-retarded Texas Death Row inmate whose death sentence was commuted to life] ring any bells? He, too, for years said this, he worked in the factory. News outlets would show him at work with his tools, and amongst other. The plan was to cancel all of this, as "mitigation" for us on death row. But, how could this be done without the outcry of the public and death row sympathizers? Cause and effect?! There was a newer prison built for death row, which is called the Estell Unit, maximum! But this was too harsh, they didn't want to appear to do us inhumanely. Unless something happened and then all sympathy would be out the window. There were, too, the squabbles with the political side of this thing, we'd still be residing in Huntsville, and not here in Livingston where we are at now. So, the escape occurred! They, the officials, knew about it well beforehand. In fact, there were inmates who partook in this escape who were, in fact, involved in the previous escapes and should never have been on the work program. They had a serious history of assaults and disruptive behavior.

So, when they did their escape attempt, it was no question: the public was in an outcry! Then, anything they wanted to do to us was a green light! And of course the same things that contributed to that escape, still exists now . . . such as "new officers"! Death Row has long been a "training facility" for new officers. To prepare them for the real prison life. Not only was d/row then and still is a place where retirees come to work and have less fear of being attacked. This is where they came and still do, even now. So the escape was allowed to take place, which then forfeited all the privileges we had. Even though the women's death row was still allowed to work, we've been on indefinite suspension since '99.

I still managed to work after the escape. I was reclassified from Huntsville, Austin, and not on the unit, like many of the others who should never had been allowed. I'd then work not only barber, SSI; I also worked commissary! I was now working these three jobs because many men were not classified to work now, after the escape. Though I liked the work anyway. I'd do this until we were all relocated here to Livingston in March 2000! I volunteered to leave about a few days before we'd be transferred here. I wanted to adjust myself to isolation; I'd been with a cell mate for years. Now, we were about to be moved, and I helped pack all the property that would be transferred here.

I enjoyed working and spending time with others, as well as the guard who would come in and I'll never forget the look on her or his face when they'd learn that I too was a death sentenced inmate. Many new officers thought I was a general population inmate that worked on death row. They would ask, are not you scared? I'd say scared of what? To work around those guys, they would have nothing to lose?! I'd then tell them I am sentenced to die! The look would say it all, then some would say, well you're different! I'm like different how? Because I acted mannerly, and worked and politely addressed them and helped them through their jobs. Many weren't told much, just tossed on a wing, and told TROTTIE, he'll help you, show you what needs to be done. I must admit I took pride in this too. Not taking advantage of them. Though I faced verbal abuse from the fellow men, because I would not mislead them, whether that would be in telling them what we're allowed to have, the amount of food, servings, or allowing so many men out on the runway when there was an hourly in/out. We would get an hourly in/out where the floors would be opened to allow you to enter your cell for a shot of coffee, or use the bathroom, and come out the next hour, retrieve a snack or whatever. I didn't and still don't like when people are misled.

I looked at those guard's jobs as if they were mine, and they could have lost them if they did something wrong and been written up for it, based on my untruthfulness. This has its drawbacks. I was always called on to work when I would sometimes just want to relax. I was called upon because I could get the job done, right and efficiently, without dragging it out like many others did.

Fast Forward: March 3, 2000, Arrived at Terrell/Polunsky Unit

This experience was much more worse than arriving to death row back in December 1993! We all were chained and shackled like beasts, slaves! We were made to sit down on the ground, place our feet together, and our hands clasped in front, with our knees bent. The shackles would be placed on in this position, so when you stood up, you'd be hunched over, and walked in a hunched-over downward wobble! This is how we were all chained like wild beasts and relocated from Ellis One to Terrell Unit, as it's formerly known, by the businessman who this unit was named after, had it changed. He didn't want his name associated with death row, so it was renamed to A.B. Polunsky, after another board member of the Texas prison system. As we made the journey here, I thought I'd never in my life miss a prison! I'd heard stories about this one, and though I looked forward to a "new" beginning, from the start nothing seemed to be good looking. We'd been promised that once all of d/row was relocated here, to this more secure prison then we'd regain all of our privileges, work program etc. But we all were misled! We're still waiting now! Well, at least I am, that is.

They said that we had to be shackled like that because, the first fifty guys who were involved in the escape, and other "worst of the worst" were already shipped here about a month, actually six months before all d/row would follow. But again they were the worst of the worst, bad actors. But our former president George W. Bush wanted all of us to be treated so alike because it was a huge embarrassment for him to have a huge escape from a maximum security prison! So now, all is allowed to be done to death row that would not otherwise have been tolerated.

As we arrived here, for what seemed like about a two-hour ride, we turned the corner and saw the prison off in a distance, much more modern than I'd seen any before. When we entered the parking lot, there were towers and guards all standing out in show of force, they knew we were headed here, and the unit was locked down. There were guys here already, death row along with general population inmates, Administrative Segregation inmates. This place was rocking and rolling because Administrative Segregation would wire the d/row guys up! This place was a living hell! It's unofficial name was Terrell the Terror Dome! Many lives were lost here, and the mentality of those guards from those inmates still resonates within us. The prison has a curse on its name. They'd quickly relocated all the other Administrative Segregation men from here to other prisons and some to Ellis where we'd just left. They quickly slapped a coat of paint on the walls in the cells and changed out the mattresses and pillows. I got off the bus, from the ride, and my wrists were cut from the black box used for the shackles and chains. I waddled off and was stripped right there; there were WOMEN all over the place! More women then we'd left at Ellis, and Ellis d/row had a 90 percent woman employment.

I felt raped, being stripped in front of them all, as they watched me with stares, not sure of their stares at my manhood, or at the scar from my knee to groin in my inner thigh from the bullet that tore through my main artery. Looks like a massive shark bite, I'd tell most who asked what happened! Then later tell the truth. After getting some boxers, because they didn't give us any on the way over, they were placed inside a brown bag and shipped with other property, we just had jumpers on. Once asked what size we wore, this would be the size we'd be given when necessary. Then I was escorted down this semi-long hallway, off to the sides are the pods, there's six pods total. I was escorted to D-Pod, which is the pod I'm currently on now.

When we made the left turn toward the door to enter the pod, the two guards escorting me, handcuffed in front, pressed a button that signaled the picket officer's attention to open the door. When they stepped to the side to see who rang the bell, they pushed a button and the door opened, that's when the NOISE! Unbelievable noise screamed out at me! It somewhat scared me. It was just crazy, there were so many reverberations, just echoing all over the place. It took me years to adjust to the echoing of this building. I'd find myself having to scream just to talk to be heard. I was escorted to E-Section #62 cell. As I walked by a section, that would be F-section, I heard my name being called. I couldn't tell where it was coming from; it echoed like crazy. I didn't want to look off because I wanted to stay focused on where I was going. When they stepped in front of #62 cell it automatically opened from the picket officer's controls. I stepped inside this spacious cell, with super bright illuminating light! When the door closed behind me, I nearly jumped to the bunk, because the sound of it crashing was deafening! Something that I still can't get used to now, years later, when certain guards make it their point to crash this door open or closed. There's this sound that's triggered by traumatic gunshots when I faced those bullets tearing through my body. I'd become enraged and often had trouble sleeping at night, even when it was another cell that was being opened/closed.

When the food slot was opened, using a steel bar, about the size of a bar used for free weights, but maybe two feet long, I would bend down, way down, almost lose my balance! This was much lower then what we were used to. I wondered, why was this so low to the ground. It was difficult for the much larger, fatter men to squat this low and hold this position until the guards would cuff you or uncuff you. They would do this on purpose too, one of the many tactics I'd learn to observe that this place is designed for. After having the cuffs removed, the closing of this food slot would be too a deafening sound! Metal to metal! Nothing but echoing and on the inside of this larger cell, it really rang in your ears. We'd get our property later. Many men lost much of theirs, typewriters damaged, legal materials lost or just discarded. Many years of legal material lost, deliberately and some mistakenly.

Life on Death Row on Terrell/Polunsky Unit

After studying my new surroundings and trying to get a sense of this madness, it was overwhelming for me. I wanted to cry! Really! This was much more traumatic then when I first arrived to death row some seven years earlier. The cell was a huge one, not larger than the cells on the work program, which was basically a four-man cell, but we used it as a two-man cell. This was indeed much more spacious than the single cells at Ellis. It even looked cleaner! I'd learn that it wasn't so later. As I looked around, which is a habit, to search any new housing, in case something was left deliberately and returned to claim it was yours, I've seen this set-up on others. There was NO WINDOW! Except for a small slit! About as wide as your palm, from the base of your hand to where your fingers start and about three feet long. I can't see out of it unless I stand up on something. I roll my mattress up and stand on it to look out only to see other eyes staring back at me from the pod. I'd later find out to be F-pod. They had known we were coming because they were on lock down and this was how some guys know how to send signals to each other from pod to pod.

I immediately got cold! From the moment I stepped inside, because there was this super forcefully blowing ventilation vent that was blowing so hard that I couldn't hear the guys calling out my name who were on the bus with me, and placed in other cells. This thing sounded like a turbine wind tunnel. We got here in MARCH so it was still somewhat chilly outside and this ventilation was or is air/water cooled. It was like a freezer. I'm standing there with a jumper on, with no sleeves, the jumpers at d/row had sleeves, I immediately noticed that these on this unit were sleeveless and all the jumpers that were transferred here would later have their sleeves cut off: Why? What's the first thing you do when you're cold, place your hands on both your arms, like giving yourself a hug. The sleeves were a little longer which hang down to your elbow. So without any sleeves, you're cold! Another psychological tactic I'd later identify here.

The light was so bright, I started to get a headache from it. Though not sure if it was from the lighting, the echoing noises, the cold wind or what?! There's a single two socket outlet and a single operation light switch, where you push the button in, light comes on, push once more and light goes off. The light is like what you'd find in your typical department store, or school, the fluorescent. Though it's not on the roof, like they're supposed to be, but standing vertically, and directly in your face, which when it comes on it wakes you from your sleep! That bright! Though in 2002, they were replaced by a much brighter lighting with a mirror inside to reflect the brightness, plus a small night light was also on these new lights. However they never replaced the double switch which allows us to use the night light and not the super bright light. We did have personal night lamps at Ellis, but coming here, all that changed. We're now Administrative Segregation!

Things we had at Ellis are now deemed contraband! Nail clippers, contraband, Elmer's glue, just to name a few of the childish things we can't have. They just allowed us to buy a night lamp this year. 2008, which is about money! They were provided by the prison at Ellis. NOW standardized toothbrushes are deemed contraband, if you've got one you can keep it until it's no good. I've been using the same one for years! The ones they sell now are the length of your THUMB! Really! Those lead to premature teeth decaying by not being able to reach your back teeth. Thus, yet another tactic I've learned that involves mental torture here.

There are two vents in the cell, the top vent blows in air, and the bottom vent which is smaller sucks out the stale air, the entire system is re-circulating. Forced air, not a/c, but climate controlled and that is it. We'd learn the first summer we were here. As they turn the air off, so they claimed it was broken, and we were in these heat boxes! Guys who had fans burned up! The oil we could have for our fans was taken and deemed contraband. There was no circulating air, it was terrible! It was so hot the walls were sweating . . . that I would later learn too, that they do this somewhat regularly, where it's so humid inside the floor sweats in the cell as well out on the runway where officers can't walk.

Years later I'd discover that this is what led to the massive build up of mold! The newly painted walls would peel from the heat, thus exposing the feces-stained walls from the men who occupied the cells days before us. This place was a madhouse and its evidence was now beginning to show and smell! The cell door is almost solid, but for two slits as about the same size as my window that looks outside, though this is a screened opening. This thing was awashed in feces as well, just quickly rinsed off, but the shit was never scrubbed off! It was just terrible!

BREAKING NEWS!!! I just heard on the news that a d/row inmate's mother was arrested at an Austin airport because her son had a cell phone here in the prison that she was paying for the minutes on. And how they found out is that he'd lent the phone out to several guys and one of them called Senator Whitmire!!! Though those cell phones have been caught here in the prison d/row for more than a year now. But I guess someone let the cat out of the bag when they called the Texas senator! They didn't say who the inmate was who called the senator, nor, how the phone was smuggled into the prison. Maybe this could be a good thing. First of the year Texas prisons will install pay phones for inmate's usage. However Administrative Segregation and d/row will not have access. The reason it was given why Texas Department of Criminal Justice was allowing pay phones because too many confiscations of cell phones. Now, there's been several here on death row alone! I'm wondering if we will be entitled to this as well? Who would need them moreso than us?! Trying to call lawyers who don't reply back to letters or come visit, etc. I heard the price for a cell goes for $1,500 a pop! For me it's not worth it, and not for me. It's cheaper for letters. But with the warden always restricting our postage which he's not supposed to, then no wonder guys are resorting to other means. I suspect we'll be on lock down for some time. We went on lock down October 13. This could be a longer ride this time.

So it's a constant fight for the fight of your life to save your life from your appeals and then from the poor quality of our environment. I won't even go into the food, which is another essential life preservement. Many changes have been made to this unit since we've been here, mostly security enhancements, from the super bright lights, to an extra sheet of steel metal over the lights, another sheet of metal attached to the bottom of the cell doors, extra locks on the pipe chases, most recent this year, some stadium lights that surround this building, to an airport X-ray machine inside this building. Not to forget the thousand dollar or more "electric fencing" that surrounds this building. So many upgrades have been made to this unit when it comes to security, but nothing has been done to repair the structure, interior, that has to do with quality of life. But what do they really care? We're here to die, and if that means any way other than lethal injection, then so be it!

What is a day like here on Texas death row? During a typical day, when we are not on lockdown like now, it will start like this, shift changes at about 5:45 a.m., the first shift officers will count about 6 a.m. At this time they will ask and or set up the first round of recreation, there's two tiers, top row and bottom row. The days alternate who goes out to recreation the first round. They will start in the first section, which is A-section, and set up the first round, go to the next cell and set up the second round and maybe the third round, come into the next section through a crossover door, and first cell, he's asked if he's going to recreation. If so, he'll get ready, if not, they'll go to the next cell and ask him if he is going to recreation? This will be repeated around the entire pod on that row whichever is first. There are some cases where an entire row will refuse! Then, the guard will start on the top row with the first cell.

The dayrooms are only about four feet from the cells, each section has their own dayroom, and there are outside yards. They are closed in without roofs, which gives you some sun, rain as well. When it's raining you are still put outside unless you refuse your recreation. Unlike at Ellis, you went to recreation and still had the option of going outside or staying inside in the dayroom. Here, if it's your outside day, which alternates, and it's raining, freezing, you're put outside in this bad weather. With a jacket that's not waterproof. Same in summer as the hot sun beats down on you there's no place for any shade. There used to be some weights. But each six months or year, a new warden or major comes to oversee death row, and they take more and more. We've been through several wardens, captains, and majors! Not to mention the lower level staff. From sergeants to lieutenants on up the rank and file. No one wants to accept responsibilities.

What is Life Like on Death Row???

We went from one hour of recreation to two hours. At first it was one hour seven days a week, then it changed to two hours five days a week. Each section has its alternate days that the section will not get to recreation. No one recreates on Sundays, unless there is a situation where that section is stuck out, like with bad weather. They'll let us make it up on a Sunday, but that depends on the ranking supervisor. Dayroom is nothing more than a large enclosed area that has a table with four seats, a chin-up bar and a thin exercise mattress. Also, inside this dayroom is a combo toilet and sink. We're recreated alone. There are no board games provided to death row inmates, though this is a common thing for other inmates who are not Administrative Segregation. We can't get them although our taxes from the commissary purchases that inmates make goes to funding these board games. The dayroom is about four feet from the cells, depending on where your cell is on the run, some are farther way from the dayroom.

I prefer to leave away from the dayroom. Because each time someone comes into the dayroom that immediately wants to talk to you, you could find yourself conversing with each inmate that comes to the dayroom every two hours! They all want to talk. Some will bring their own purchased board games to the dayroom, such as chessboard or dominoes and they will play with the guy that lives in the closest cell. With dominoes, they will place them on or in the bars facing the cell where the inmate can see them and tell the other what to play. This can be played on the floor from inside the dayroom, or at the table, if the inmate can see good enough from his cell to the table. With chess, all they do is holler out their moves.

The dayroom can be an area where you're targeted by other inmates and tier assaults. The cell doors are solid except with the two screened windows. Inmates who are feuding with another can shoot spears at the inmate in the dayroom. The dayroom is an "opened" enclosure with regular bars. It's not closed in with mesh wire, like the one that's located down on F-pod. F-pod is where those offenders who have been disciplined are sent to do their restrictions.

You can be targeted for any reason. Whether you don't wish to pass anything from one dayroom to the other. This is how inmates are able to share things between themselves. Such as books, magazines, or, more importantly, legal work. The dayrooms are opened cages where one inmate can throw something to the next inmate in the other dayroom. When an inmate wishes to not participate in these daily activities he'll be subject to verbal abuse as well as assaults by way of him being pelted with either liquids or spears shot at him from the cells closest to the dayroom. This has long been known to be a risk. When former gang members were housed in these cells. This could also take place when the inmate is escorted to the shower and back. He can be assaulted then, even though the two escorting guards with him are his "shield" protector. They often don't follow the procedures, and one guard will be standing at your cell door, whilst the other is escorting you from or to the shower.

At the Ellis unit, there was a shield, Plexiglas that the guard would walk with you behind this shield. It was rolled on a track. However this shield was on only two wings and these were the wings where assaultive inmates were housed. There were not on the other wings, and they had open bars where the inmates could reach out and touch you. But, there wasn't any violence at Ellis. All the violence has taken place here, mostly inmates on other inmates. Which many will not go to recreation. I prefer to go outside. It's a one on one, I'm in a single man yard, the guy is in the other yard. Just the two of us. A decent conversation without yelling to be heard. Unlike in the dayrooms, you cannot have a single conversation because everyone's calling you for your help, to pass something, or you have to yell over to the next guy to have a conversation or be heard. When you're in a dayroom, you have to entertain fourteen other guys because they're all knocking for your attention.

Outside, there's nothing more than a chin-up bar, a basketball and goal, and a latrine. There used to be some weights on one side of the yard. They were removed for the obvious. They kept us healthy, and in shape. Nothing more than a simple contraption that was about maybe 130 pounds and a single bar with two plates welded at the ends, welded into a rack on the wall. You could do nothing more but dead lifts, squats, that's it, no other movement by this contraption. It was effective in keeping you in shape, legs wise. When you're lying down for more than twenty-two hours a day. I didn't start shooting basketball until those weights were removed. I had stopped going outside altogether before I began to shoot the ball. I was depressed. Now, I look forward to shooting the ball.

Special Memories From My Past: Funny, Sad, Frightening

There's many memories from my past, and I'm not sure how to organize them or express them in like fashion.

Special memories of my beloved wife and our son, how we'd be together and enjoy ourselves, traveling from Texas to Louisiana, family gatherings. Special memories of my wife and I, when we'd go to amusement parks and ride the highest ride and she would hold me and hug my body tightly. Of our special meetings at designated places, where she'd enjoy eating her tacos, and I'd have my chicken fried steak.

Most of the times, we'd be working and just show up at each other's job for lunch and have a good time enjoying each other's company, or I'd surprise her with her favorite meal. The memories of our son being born about a week and a half before Thanksgiving. I was truly thankful for his birth, though it was a rocky one and life threatening. He's huge as ever. Our first Christmas together. Our Easter and though it was a short time, they're special.

Frightening memories was when I would be ushered into a foster home with people I've never seen before or knew. I'd run away from each home they'd place me into, to track my mother down, each time to be sent back to another home, until they tired of me running away and allowed me to stay with my mother. But then my Dad would be working behind the scenes, and he'd come to reclaim his kids and we'd be whisked away to another state and with family members who were just like strangers too! But those were some wonderful times and saddening times. All those events shaped my psyche, how I didn't want my son to go through what I did as a child. God was with me through all those adventures, even now.

Frightening would be from the experiences of my son's complicated birthing, from his surgery at a weight of only three pounds or less. The shock of being shot multiple times and actually seeing it happen before my own eyes. It was like an out of body experience.

Funny times when we'd imitate our favorite singers, my wife and I, and sing their songs. We did this of course in our own homes.

Funny thing: Seeing the expression of a guard's face, when they learned that I was a death row inmate too, who had worked with them for a week or the first day. They'd heard so many stories about d/row. And, they had to be reprogrammed all over again. They will be programmed as they come through the academy, watching videos, of past/present inmates who acted out, so these images were in their minds, until they walked the runways of death row and saw it was like a puppy's kennel! Same would occur when I'd be taken to dental office and sitting next to a general population inmate and he asked, how long you've got? I told him I'm d/row! He looked at me like I've got the plague! When I've run across some guard who would come to the place I'd worked security before. They're like it's unbelievable, you're the same guy?! Can't be! Expressions!

Special memories of my step-daughter learning to ride her bike! Seeing the smiles on the kid's faces when I volunteered for x-mas functions and brought them toys or food! Even when I sat with elders at homes for them, just to be in their company, feelings of a loved one, child, sibling, relative, etc. Soooo many.

Sorry I don't have much to share on this particular topic. I do have many, they are just buried back down deep under the years of sadness here, and loneliness.

Reflections

When I reflect back on my life before arriving on D/Row, I think of awaking in the early morning hours, embracing my family and off to a good days' work. I long for the days to be able to work and make a living from a paying job. Providing for myself. I reflect back on lunch breaks, being able to sit with a co-worker at a place of business enjoying a drink with an iced tea. I remember getting off work and rushing home to pick my son up and hold him dear to my heart, as well as my wife and daughter if she wasn't working. Doing the things a parent loves and enjoys doing with family.

I recall the family gatherings we'd have with lots of food and music playing kids running all over the place and being joyous. Seeing how everyone has grown since the last gathering. I reflect back on the days when they were either Houston hot and humid or cold and freezing out, I loved them all, and no matter the weather conditions I was looking forward to another day of work to provide for the customers that relied on our services. Whether that was in working at the auto parts store or shipping/handling/loading tractor trailers with hospital supplies that some injured patient needed. Or, when I worked security some place where people could come and enjoy themselves and feel safe as well. Just making an honest and decent living to provide for family. Reflecting back on all special events, whether someone's birthday or a holiday. Most importantly, I reflect back on how God was then and still able now to care for me and protect me. Even now. With his undying love and mercies.

Oftentimes I find myself feeling sorrow for myself, the pain that's caused for my families and in-laws and those of my friends. Those kids who are now young adults. I pray that their lives were not severely altered from my actions. Sure, any time a loved one is absent that life is altered. But as I've learned too, life still goes on, God still has plans for those shattered lives and only He can make it better within ourselves.

To help me cope and deal with this daily pain of sorrow and defeat, I pray to God, and seek His awesome strength and guidance daily. I not only reflect back on what I didn't, but all of what God has done and shown me when I was free and since being confined to death row. In essence He's shown me I am still free! My spirit and mind, conscience. Each morning, I awake, I offer God my sincere prayers and thanks for blessing me with another day, and to help me through this day with kindness to others. Yet, I've learned since not to really focus on the past, but what's still ahead. And not so much as my planned and possible execution but the plentiful mercies that God blesses me with on a daily basis, and from year to year.

Observations

There have been many I've made over the past fifteen years on d/row. Those many of myself. However, living amongst and in close quarters with others, it's also well observed of others. Often I ask why or how come? For the most part, it's a gradual change for some, and then for others it's a lifetime and then, well, no one never gets it.

Looking back at who I was, and what I stood for, my morals really have remained the same because I was brought up in a way that's still to moral society standards. Work hard for what you want for yourself and families. Be honest and don't swindle the next guy. Treat others as you would want to be so treated. Most if not all of those rules or traditions go out the window when one enters prison, and for that matter so for death row! It's a daily struggle to not be conformed to the majority of mindsets who you're surrounded by. Though if you weren't strong minded before, you will definitely be led astray and taken advantage of by prisoners and guards alike.

If you're not criminal minded, you will be because the urge and normal daily life here is to fit in, get along with others. However I buck this trend daily. Again if you were weak minded before you came to prison you will become criminal minded and accept the ways of others and prison life and mentality, get over anyway you can, look out for self before anyone else. However, it's relevant why so many prison gangs are formed and people joined. Not only from physical protection but from mental, psychological bullying. That can come from guards as well. Because the power to control is so overwhelming for those who can't dispense it evenly and fairly.

Life is indeed a learning lesson and for some, the little things that should've been learned early on weren't. Or they were seriously misinterpreted. I find myself struggling against the forces of evil, the wrong doers, to lead others in the right direction. That's with guards and inmates alike. But I look for no accolades from others and don't mind being looked at as non-convict! Though I've been wrongly convicted, I am not a convict! As it's used to symbolize prison status or worthiness.

With the current prison population as it is, I know why so many return to prison. If d/row's any indication of the general population mentality then it's obvious why so many return. A majority of d/row are first timers in prison. A majority however have been in juvenile lock ups before, and the other half were former prisoners. I, myself, am a first timer all the way around. But after years of interacting and close observations one concludes that many just haven't gotten it yet. Drugs are a major factor, and so is greed. Wanting the fast and easy money, not the hard and toiled sweat two weeks paycheck. And then there's the subgroup like myself, emotional and family-related crimes.

One thing I've learned, and after careful studying of my daily strength and God's work, is that nothing man does now hasn't been done before. All is vanity, fleeting with time. Just like man himself. He should give thanks daily for his many blessings, health, life, family and all that he's got. God will provide all else. I failed in this respect because I was working and working but neglected to give thanks. I foolishly thought all that I did and obtained was from my own hard work and toil. Self-pride is another destroyer of self and His blessings. Taking things for granted, not really realizing what you have been blessed with until it's taken from you in a flash. I'm like the man Lazarus who was in the comforting arms of Moses' bosom, and the other man who lived good and full, and when he died he was tormented, and he wanted someone to tell his brother's family what to do, and not end up where he was tormenting in hell. I try to reach others, and give them the heads up to give thanks, praise God sincerely, take time from your busy schedules and share with family. The things we take for granted. Love, love, and love. Don't harbor resentment of others.

I've observed that I've matured in the sense of my priorities and my compassion for others because God has compassion for me! I've learned to forgive others, when I'm desiring my victim's family to forgive me. We should more importantly repent and seek God's forgiveness as well, and those who we have hurt. I have observed that the world and life is nothing more than a repeated cycle, like the seasons. With generations and those generations not being well educated and loved, thus this breeds the violence that permeates this society now. The cycle is not broken. A person hurting wants another to be hurting as well, and that hurting cycle repeats and repeats itself thus making generations worse and worse. So from my love and concern, I try to stop this cycle by sharing what I know now, but didn't back then, to those I know and love to not repeat the cycle. That is done in here as well, and I pray that the cycle of hate and violence will come to an end. Sure, it will, from a scripture standpoint, at the return of Jesus! That I believe! But I also believe that we can now stop this cycle as well. Those who seriously wish to.

I'll end this here and thank you for allowing me to partake in this expression of who I am, and not what I'm alleged to be by the state that wishes to end my life! But my life's in God's hands . . . and if it's His will that it be ended, then so be it, Thy Will Be Done!!!

Sincerely,
Willie "T-Rock" Trottie

Gaylon Walbey, Jr.
#999114

Age: 34
Hometown: Houston
Last school: Reagan, Houston, Texas
Education: Ninth grade
Interests: *[Names Withheld], automobile design, product design, marketing, artistry, music production, going home*
Favorites: *Cars - 2009 Camaro, Chrysler 300C, Tesla Roadster; Books -* Celestine Prophecy, Cosmic Test Tube, A Friendship With God; *Song - "All My Life" by KC and JoJo*

Favorite Quotes

—You miss one hundred percent of the shots you don't take. – Wayne Gretsky

—If you control yourself and your behavior other people will treat you with respect, eliminate any reason for conflict. – Chuck Norris

—If you want to succeed, increase your failure rate. – IBM Founder, Thomas Watson

—It is said that revenge is sweet . . . so is rat poison.

—Don't follow your dreams . . . hunt them down! – Bud Brutsman

—Nobody can make you feel inferior without your consent. – Eleanor Roosevelt

—Women fake orgasms. But men fake whole relationships. —Sharon Stone

—You know a tree by the fruit it bears. —Anonymous

—Nothing in the world can take the place of persistence. Talent will not; nothing is more common than unsuccessful men with talent. Genius will not; unrewarded genius is almost a proverb. Education will not; the world is full of educated derelicts. Persistence and determination are omnipotent. —Calvin Coolidge

—If nothing ever changed, there'd be no butterflies. —Anonymous

—Yes we can. —Barack Obama

Dear World,

Just yesterday, America elected her first black president in a record breaking, landslide victory. As a thirty-four year old black man on Texas' death row, I don't have the right and can't possibly be proud, because his position doesn't make me look good due to the fact that my position makes him look bad.

He's an archetype.
I'm a stereotype.

I am thoroughly ashamed of myself. I have been on Texas' Death Row (DR) since '94. I didn't know I could draw or design until I got locked up for this case. It was as a homeless eighteen year old with a thirteen year old mind and psychological disorders like schizophrenia that I attempted my first robbery of my former foster mother, which turned deadly. Killing her was not part of my plan. I'm still trying to sort through what happened and why. I am sorry to her, her family, her friends, and the community.

Because this murder was not premeditated, it is not a capital murder case, so by law, I don't even qualify for the death penalty. Furthermore, the only way to get to Texas death row is to be a future danger—not revenge, not eye for an eye, and not because one deserves it. Future dangerousness is the only criteria: Texas death penalty law is preemptive, not punitive. Period.

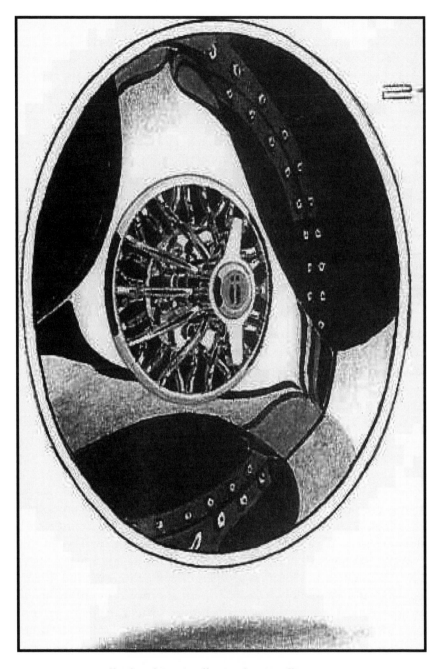

"Wheel Design" - Gaylon Walbey, Jr.

So if there's no violence on my record before nor during these fifteen years. After the crime, how am I a future danger? This is also my first conviction. Yes, it's that easy to put someone on death row. You need only scar (and scare) a jury with gruesome details.

I've done my time for what I did (fifteen years flat of Death Row time). It's time for me to go home to my family . . . the following is but part of the reasons for my release.

For a strategic policy of anonymity, I threw away the Texas Review Press' initial call for entries for this book. I regretted doing so after several subsequent pivotal transpirations in my life. At any time between 2003 and today I could have taken my story to the media, but for many reasons, I did not want the attention. Today, I have no choice but to do so before certain golddiggers angle and mangle my story, as well as to preserve and protect what rightfully belongs to two other people and myself.

And by a miracle of sorts I received a follow-up letter from TRP today. That's why I pray.

Along with this story, I am providing many of my drawings and photos as well as some of my unreleased designs for the world to witness firsthand that I am the original designer and the rights belong to me. Many are poised to steal my work and take credit for it (and money) as this continues to happen over and over again and I'm tired of it. Simple.

The last straw was actually yesterday when I received the latest *Lowrider Magazine* in the mail. It was in a wheel advertisement for "Giovanna Forged 2 Piece" that I immediately spotted one of my unreleased wheel designs, which they named "F-16." Giovanna is a brand in a sea of over 15,000 other wheel designs on the market that is the only one that looks like that, which is difficult to do in a monkey-see-monkey-do market. However, last year I authorized one like that to be released, as I've done many similar to it. Though the two are obviously siblings, they are as different as boy and girl.

Nevertheless, "F-16" is a stolen design and I intend to get my credit for the breakthrough design it is and the money [name withheld] owes me for it. I have an idea which thief gave it to them, but I'm not sure. This happens to me frequently; I could call out many other companies who not only have stolen designs of mine, but who also pirate my designs I have released on the market. There are over 300 wheel companies in the U.S. with over 15,000 designs on the market. I am the most imitated designer in the game and the most underpaid simultaneously, and I'm sick of it. It's time for me to get my dues.

As of this writing, my authorized released designs are in the company called [name withheld], which makes the Dub brand, under which most of my designs are concentrated. The owner and members of his family have been here from California to visit me many times. His wife has written me letters and he has sent me over one hundred Fed Exes since 2003. Since 2003 I have sent him over 4,500 solicited wheel designs.

Rides Magazine did interviews with the top five wheel companies. The following is an excerpt of the interview:

Rides: You have been the first or one of the first to debut more than one trend. How do you consistently stay ahead of the curve?

[name withheld]: It's all about working with people who are enthusiastic with what they do. Like the designer "Dubman" who helped me get Dub off the ground. I saw that he had a consistent style. He wouldn't just go draw anything. (Dec/Jan '08 issue, Page 117).

He is speaking of me; I am known as Dubman, because I am the designer of the megapopular dub wheels made by [name withheld].

To those familiar with Dub, yes, I am that guy, the one and only. I am Dubman. For those unfamiliar with the wheel game, you will never again see any wheel the same.

The wheel designs are totally unique and original. Due to no fault of my own, Texas Department of Criminal Justice stopped allowing me to order supplies from art stores. The only art supplies in TDCJ's commissary are preschool watercolors, preschool colored pencils, low quality drawing paper and illustration boards. Hence, my drawings are rendered with #2 pencils, black prison issue writing pens and colored pencils.

I have no access to computers or high end software—haven't even seen a TV in over eight and a half years since they took all TVs from death row in 2000. It was in 2006 that they stopped me from ordering drawing paper from stores, so bear with being on America's most administratively oppressive death row for fifteen years. (This is the only death row in America without TVs.)

Being on death row leaves me totally vulnerable because I have no way of protecting myself or my family. All I can do is compromise, sacrifice, and beg, and I'm tired of it. I am at everyone's mercy because of my limitations and my position.

I have a gift, which means no matter what my conditions are or how bad things get or how much people try to hold me back, my true nature is to innovate. Thus, as long as I'm in prison, I suspect, people will continue to steal my innovations because as long as I have been in prison, people have continued to steal my innovations. In the process, people also continue to try to cross [name withheld] out, because she's the only person in this world I trust. She's earned that trust over nine and a half years. She clears the bases when she's up to bat. She's my everything.

One of Barack Obama's books is called "The Audacity of Hope." I have just given you a snippet of my life on Texas Death Row in words, drawings, photos, and ideas. It's not too audacious to hope that I might be a budding archetype in a stereotype's clothing, is it?

Sincerely,
Gaylon

Daryl Wheatfall
#999020

Age: *43*
Hometown: *Houston*
Last school: *Jones High School, Houston*
Education: *Eleventh grade*
Interests: *Reading, writing, music*
Favorites: *Books* - The Confession of Nat Turner, *George Orwell's* 1984, The Story of John Brown: Cloud Splitter, Roots

Acknowledging Reality (from *InCaged*, March/April 2007)

InCaged wishes to acknowledge the influences that reality, people, places, and major events have on how we think and feel, affects our decisions, how we view one thing from another, or the impact reality or illusion has upon society and how it shapes society's ideology and beliefs. 'Ideology'—a very interesting word. It means a body of ideas reflecting social needs, aspirations of an individual, a group, a class, culture and doctrines, beliefs which form the basic political and economic makeup of an individual reality.

This is what it's all about: political and economic makeup of what reality is for you. Some of you may object or be offended that *InCaged* seeks to free you psychologically from your stereotypical prison, which has imprisoned individuals all around the world, conditioning them to accept realities of false facts due to ignorance, as well as manipulatory and subliminal injected circumstances.

Had I been giving a manifesto when I made these comments, someone in the audience may have yelled out: "Who are you? You don't know what I am, don't know anything about me, to say one way or the other!" It wasn't and isn't my intention to insult anyone. Please forgive me if I have.

"InCaged" - Daryl Wheatfall

Please consider I'm a prisoner who's been confined inside a cage all day, every day for the past sixteen years. All I do is stare out past my prison walls, looking out at society, moving by fast as the people go about living their everyday lives. Witnessing life is what I do; now please consider the name of this editorial: "Acknowledging Reality." There's no need for me to personally know you. I'm making a general observation based on society's reality as a whole. It's no different from lying on my back observing birds and their habits, voicing my opinions on their interactions! To answer your question: Who am I?

An innocent prisoner activist, sitting on death row for a crime I didn't commit. I've been abandoned by most of my family. I've been abused by this system in more ways than I care to explain, inside my sixteen years of incarceration. Beaten by guards while handcuffed. Set up by prison officials where I was stabbed close to forty times. Had to hurt a prison guard to prevent another attack on my life. Prison officials have gassed me so many times I lost count. The attacks don't stop here. I must do battle with the psychological assaults from all of this; the assaults which attack with each hour, day, month, week and year I watch pass by, separated from my family and friends.

Whenever the thought hits, I have to endure the emotional sorrow of not seeing my mother in sixteen years. As I struggle with the thought that my mother doesn't care, the thought shakes me up mentally. Being on death row, I'm looked upon as the worst of the worst! When I'm not! As if I didn't have enough to deal with, I'm forced to witness men lose their minds, watch them face death, their loved ones break down in sorrow as they walk away to be murdered—by the people who murder and kill prisoner after prisoner as if it's just another day at the office! Not caring anything about the next prisoner who takes that dead prisoner's place, all are killed in the name of justice. Without my faith to hold me together, I couldn't tell you who I am; with the power of the Spirit in me, I'm no different from Lazarus.

Lying at the gate of the rich, body and mind suffering, covered with sores as the dogs lick them. With each article I put out, it's as if I'm begging for crumbs, anything for the rich to hear my cries and the cries of others coming from death row. Surely I'll die. Then it will be too late for the rich who would not listen to ask Father Abraham for mercy. There'll be no dipping of a finger in water to cool your tongues—for there is a great gulf fixed between you and me. Those who would pass from hence to you cannot, neither can you pass to us. Does this tell you who I am?

The Misinformed

No matter what I just described to you, as long as manipulatory circumstances are injected into the consciousness of society, false facts will continue revealing a delusional reality. Which explains why I continue receiving comments from ignorant individuals filled with disdain and negativity just like an email I received on January 4, 2007 ("Did he care much about the living conditions of the people he killed?"). The person who sent me this has accepted the delusional reality possessing contempt against me when the only thing he knows about me is that I'm a death row prisoner. This automatically in his eyes makes me a killer because in this person's mind the justice system is never wrong. This emphatically emphasizes/defines the manipulatory circumstances dictating the beliefs and emotional feelings of the person who sent me the email.

This is why I'll use the reality of Hollywood and its movies to point out how subliminal and false facts are used to condition people's thinking, unconsciously indoctrinating them with a stereotypical concept surrounding how they view their reality. Hollywood is a culture of films seen through television and on the big screen by people all around the world. When the public watches movies like *The Exorcist*—first released in 1973, which had its audiences screaming, running scared to the closest exit after witnessing a young girl possessed by a demon—they got scared because it was believable, just like the word 'death row' signified inside the mind of our email sender that I'm a killer.

For those making movies, all they want is for you to believe it's real, even if it's only for a moment. Movies like *Psycho*, released in 1960, touch on reality. Norman Bates, motel clerk, devoted son, serial killer, running about in granny's drawers. Or *The Silence of the Lambs*, released in 1991, Mr. Hannibal Lecter himself. A very intelligent psycho killer who enjoyed eating people.

Oh, let's not forget my favorite Mr. Max Cady in *Cape Fear*, also released in 1991, about an ex-con wrongfully sentenced to prison. His court-appointed lawyer failed to correctly represent him. Released, Max is filled with malice and malpractice on his mind and goes after his lawyer who stood by ignoring his duties.

All these movies send subliminal messages, projecting an illusional reality yet based on the society surrounding us. Believable situations are identified in our everyday life. We're being conditioned to judge and associate people and situations by the characters. His or her characteristics or behaviors resemble what we've seen on TV. Unconsciously it's why the public accepts manipulatory facts given by trusted public officials and media outlets without knowing if what's being told to you is the truth.

As a whole, most of society has already been imprisoned in your own stereotypical cage, lost within the illusion which has been subliminally planted. It's why death row prisoners and myself are perceived as being no better than the evil, scary Chucky doll in the movie *Child's Play*, released in 1988-2004, a madman trapped inside a doll running around exercising his disdain for another human life, killing people as easy as changing his socks.

Please, I don't want any of you to misunderstand me! I'm not trying to make all death row prisoners innocent or say that each death row prisoner is a churchgoer who is a little angel. This isn't the case. Some of guys I've spoken with have admitted their guilt to me. Some were on drugs, robbed a store only after the money, heroically provoked the shooting. Other cases need not be discussed. Nonetheless, I'm pointing out that all death row prisoners are perceived in one sense, evil killers.

Public officials and media outlets don't put out what death row prisoners have to offer; they make sure all are placed in the same twisted company as Jason Voorhees, the murderous killer in *Friday the 13th*. A possessed killer who creates an anxiety social disorder by running around killing teenagers with a machete. It's here the stereotypical seed lives, you become possessed with this perception that all death row prisoners are killers. None are seen individually for who they are, who I am, and the principle standards they/I live by. Prisoners are released off death row all the time and never have any problem with the law.

I assure you, no one could associate me anywhere near the company of Jason Voorhees, a cold-blooded killer without a conscience, nor any other killer. Yet prisoners are seen as identical to Jason. This is what prevents the public from acknowledging the abuse, the inhumane living conditions, and the injustice happening behind these walls. And within the judicial system where guilt and innocence is decided by how much money a person has or the color of his or her skin, the truth isn't important! Judges, prosecutors, and police officers are violating the ethical standards that are supposed to separate them from the Max Cadys, the Norman Bates, and the Hannibal Lecters of today.

Yet everything these officials are doing is identical, making them no better than cold-blooded killers like Freddy, the twisted killer in *Nightmare on Elm Street* series, released 1984-2003. Freddy would pop up in his victim's dreams exercising his gross revenge. I see no difference when police lie, hide evidence, prosecutors train witnesses with what to say, or leave the most important facts out, as judges allow these violations to go on, just sit back and watch as manipulatory tactics are exercised. These officials are violating the very ethical standards the judicial laws are built on. Men are being abused and tortured on death row, then they're murdered in the name of justice.

Yet society is only able to associate prisoners with a killer like Jason Voorhees but isn't able to tell the difference between Jason and when the judicial system violates every rule in the book to murder.

Christopher Wilkins
#999533

Age: 40
Hometown: Houston
Last school: Cypress Creek High School, Houston, Texas
Education: Twelfth grade
Interests: Sex, Drugs, Rock-N-Roll
Favorites: Blonde hair, blue eyes
Other info: "Some people just need killing"

Robert Will
#999402

Age: 30
Hometown: Houston
Last school: Houston Community College
Education: I dropped out of high school in ninth grade, received GED, and
            went to community college two semesters.
Interests: The development and evolution of moral ideas and actions as
            civilization progresses—and how I can help peaceful coexistence
            of humanity become a reality.

A Close Friend Committed Suicide Yesterday

I'm in the saddest of sad moods. Writing even seems a vulgar thing to do, inappropriate because of what happened yesterday. I feel as if a dark cloud of sadness has filled up my cell, descended upon my senses. When I breathe I inhale this fog of despair. I can taste it on my tongue, smell its heavy stench. My skin is humid from its moisture. I blink and hold my eyes closed for a second . . . ten seconds . . . thirty seconds . . . a minute—it's still there.

I thrust my arm sideways in the air, slicing through the cloud, a space opens, it twirls, a sinister ghostly face forms and laughs mockingly in my ear. Since yesterday I've been lying to myself, my conscious mind denying it exists, my subconscious twisted, overwhelmed by a deep sadness, fighting this dismal haze, this profound abyss of pain.

There are really only two people here who I consider very close personal friends and one of them killed himself yesterday. He slit his own throat and died in his cell. He died alone in a small, cold cell of steel and concrete on Texas Death Row. 78-cell. F-pod. I've been fighting back tears all yesterday and today, but as I'm writing this I have tears in my eyes. I knew him since the day he got locked up in

Harris County jail, about seven years ago. He was arrested, charged, and sentenced for capital murder of a police officer about six months after I got locked up.

To understand what type of person he was, it's necessary to know about his case. He was eighteen when he got locked up. The night before his arrest he had an argument with his girlfriend and went out drinking, mixing alcohol with Xanax pills—a very bad combination. I can't remember all of the details, but something had happened like he came home in the middle of the night and his car was out of gas, so at 5 a.m. he took his sister's car to go to the store. She woke up and saw her car gone and called the police, thinking it was stolen. A Harris County deputy sheriff came and took the police report and then left. As he was going down the street, my friend was driving back home. He parked in his driveway and the police officer stopped his car, pulled out his gun, and ordered him to submit to arrest. My friend didn't know what was going on, but he got out and put his hands up and asked the officer what the problem was. The deputy approached him and slammed him face-first on the hood of the car. My friend pulled a gun he had on him and fired one time, hitting the officer in the head. The officer died. My friend ended up on Death Row.

We talked about his case many times, and he always expressed deep remorse for the reactionary, "heat-of-the-moment" murder he committed. He told me he made a stupid mistake, drunk and high off pills. Even though the deputy started slamming him around, he didn't blame the police officer for what he himself did.

One time, when we were in county jail, I went out to recreation early and went to talk to my friend. You should know that in county jail, recreation is a bit different; we're able to walk right up to the other guys' cells because there's no recreation cage, just rows of cells in a huge room. The doors are electronic and there are two-way speakers inside the cells so the officers can communicate with the prisoners. I was in a cell on the complete opposite side of the room from my friend, and on this particular day the officers decided to run recreation very early, at 6 a.m. I was the first to go out. Not wanting to wake others up, I slowly opened my door after it was unlocked. I quietly walked out of my cell, down the stairs and over to his cell to see if he might be awake.

When I got to his cell door I looked through the small, Plexiglas window.

"What the hell are you doing?!"

He was down on his knees in front of his desk, praying and

crying. There was a cross drawn on his wall with the name of the deputy he killed written across it. A newspaper article about the murder including a picture of the deputy was on the desk . . . .

"What the hell are you doing?!"

At first I didn't take in the whole scene.

A large percentage, if not the majority, of Mexicans and Mexican Americans are Catholic. For those of you who may not know, a lot of Latino Catholics will make what basically amounts to small little altars to pray in front of. I remember when I was younger, one of my friend's parents, who were Mexican American, had a whole wall in their room that was like an altar where the family would pray Catholic prayers. There was a huge portrait of Jesus Christ on the wall surrounded by wooden crosses and other religious iconography. In the center, there was a desk with religious candles and statues, of the Virgin Mary, and things like that. A family member might be sick and someone—or the entire family—would place a picture of them on the desk, light a prayer candle, and pray for them.

Right after I asked my friend what he was doing, I realized that he was saying a Catholic prayer for the deputy he killed. He had made a homemade altar in his cell. Wiping the tears from his eyes, embarrassed that I saw him in this very private moment, he stood up and came to the door.

"Man, I feel bad about that, you know, about the deputy–"

He and I spent awhile talking about what happened. He told me that he wasn't some hardcore killer, he had just made a very bad mistake, drunk and high off pills. Even though the officer was slamming him around, he shouldn't have shot him, that was just his instinctual reaction from being attacked. That's how he felt.

My friend was genuinely a good person who just made some bad choices in life, choices that affected him and many others. I'm still trapped in the midst of this dark cloud and it's hard to write. I just can't believe he killed himself. I don't even know what all happened, but I'll find out more and I'll write some more soon. One would think that with all the death that has been around me over these years, just one more death—even that of a close friend—wouldn't bother me all that much. I wish that was the case but it's not.

From Texas Death Row,
Rob Will

Arthur Lee Williams, Jr.
#000736

Age: 49
Hometown: Minneapolis, Minnesota
Last school: St. Cloud State University, St. Cloud, Minnesota
Education: A few credits on freshman year
Interests: Chess, animals (especially dogs), cycling, jewelry design/making, music (especially jazz), reading, history, and correspondence
Favorites: Books - Lord of the Rings trilogy by J.R.R. Tolkien;
            Music - Songs in the Key of Life by Stevie Wonder;
            Movies - classic movies as well as horror, sci-fi, and comedy;
            Authors - King, Kootnz, Butcher
Other info: Life is a journey, and there are many roads. Some people know where they want to go, and some people don't have a clue, but the journey is much improved when there's a friend to share the experience with.

Death Row was vastly different when I first arrived on May 6, 1983. Not only was it physically different—as it was located at the Ellis Unit in Huntsville—but it was different in a psychological/emotional way as well. From the time I first got arrested through the time of my trial and sentencing, I had heard things about "the Row" from guys at the Harris County Rehab who had been there. There were several factors that I knew would contribute to my "experiences" on the Row either for good or bad depending upon who I was dealing with. For one thing, I was young (only twenty-three at that time), plus I was Black. More notably, I wasn't from Texas and I had been sentenced to death for killing a cop. The fact that the guys on the Row would physically interact with each other, as well as the guards, on a daily basis meant that everyone had best be very respectful of the next man (I use the male gender specifically because, at that time, no females worked on Death Row).

Disrespect could very well lead to unpleasant, if not fatal, consequences; at least four prisoners were killed by another Death Row prisoner between 1979 and 1999 for having "offended" someone. My desire was to establish myself as being someone "serious"—someone who you didn't mess with and who wouldn't mess with you in return—and although I managed to accomplish that, to one degree or another, over the years I had to first overcome a not-so-serious initial impression on some of the guys.

I felt very fortunate that when I first arrived I was assigned to the cell right next to one of the only guys I already knew on the Row. He was a tall White guy who was from Arkansas that I had gotten to know at the Rehab as we were both going to trial in the same time period. Going through a capital murder trial is a unique experience and it was out of this that a friendship began to develop between us. He had gotten to the Row about three weeks ahead of me and so he already knew who was who and what was what. He not only looked out for me with regards to sharing information with me about how things were but was generous in providing me with hygiene and writing supplies, cigarettes (this was before the lawsuits and bans when seventy percent of the prisoners smoked and Texas Department of Criminal Justice even provided free Bull Durham rolling tobacco), sodas and snacks until I could get my commissary ticket. I was very much looking forward to being able to make my own commissary order as I noticed they had various "canned goods"—roast beef, meatballs, chili, soups, etc.—and I wanted something more "substantial" to eat besides the cookies, chips, candy bars and pastries that my friend seemed to thrive on.

Looking over the commissary listing I noticed that there was no sort of "griddle" or "hot pot" for sale, so I asked my friend what were we supposed to do in order to get our food from commissary heated up and/or cooked, and he told me that's what a "stinger" was on the list for. I had no idea of just what a "stinger" was but I ordered one anyway when I was finally able to make my first commissary order. When I got my commissary order in I immediately sat down on my bunk to check everything out. The stinger was inside of a little blue and white box that was about two inches wide, five inches long and one inch deep and the writing on the box said that it was an "immersion heating element." Okay, "immersion" means that it needs to be "immersed" so I used my brand new can opener to open up a can of chili with beans, stuck the stinger inside of the chili and plugged it into the wall socket! I'm sure some people might already see where this is going, right?

I'm sitting on the bunk telling my friend about all of the stuff that I had ordered—typewriter, radio, fan, tennis shoes, etc.—and before too long I smell something burning. The smell got so strong, so fast that guys several cells away and some above me started saying that something was burning. I turned around and saw smoke coming out of the can of chili and I immediately rushed to the back of the cell (which took me all of three steps) to unplug the stinger. The smell of burnt beans was very unpleasant and I started fussing and cussing that the commissary must have sold me a "defective" stinger. My friend asked me what happened and I told him that the stinger burnt up my chili. He asked me, "how did it do that?" And I told him, "it burnt up the chili!" as though it should be obvious as hell what I was talking about. He replied, "I don't understand. What did you do that it could burn up the chili?" And so I explained to him that I had opened up the can of chili, put the stinger inside of the chili, plugged it in and it burnt up the damned chili; I was pretty exasperated at that point!

There was a long moment of silence in the cellblock and then, all of a sudden, not only my friend but several guys in the immediate cells around us all busted out laughing. The laughter caught me by surprise as I still didn't understand what was so funny and I'm hearing comments like, "you fool" or "is you stupid" or even worse before he can, finally, control his laughter enough to tell me that I was supposed to put the can of chili in a bowl of water and then put the stinger in the water to heat up the can of chili!

For a Black man I'm sure that I must have turned a few shades of red in those first moments of understanding; talk about total embarrassment! Guys that I didn't even know—at that time—laughed and joked about this incident for several weeks, but he was the worst. He would give me "step-by-step" instructions on how to do just about anything just to clown me. I couldn't really get mad at anyone for laughing at me because, once I saw it for what it was, I thought it was pretty funny myself. However, he was enjoying himself a little too much at my expense and I was determined to make him "pay" for it!

Let me explain something to you about my friend; the guy was a "fanatic" when it came to his cell and/or his person being neat and clean. He would wash his sheets every other day, practically scrub his cell from wall to wall daily, comb his hair every twenty minutes (the guy had hair that would have made Elvis—who my friend idolized—envious of him!) and keep his personal clothing spotless. His only "bad" habits were that he smoked and loved caffeine—either hot coffee or cold Cokes. We used to have ice available to us at meal times and so I got one of the porters to bring me a large cup full of ice. I knew he would only drink a soda if he had ice for it so I took a can of Coke off my shelf, shook it up until the bottom started bulging out from the pressure, and then I knocked on the wall between our cells to get his attention and handed him the cup of ice and soda through the bars . . . he never suspected a thing!

In less than thirty seconds, I heard the pssstffoooossshhh of the pop top being pulled and THE LIQUID SPRAYING OUT and then there was the sound of his fussing and cussing; the more he cussed me out, the funnier it was to me and as guys in the cells around us figured out what happened they joined in the laughter too. It was a day or so before my friend stopped being mad at me (that's probably about how long it took him to clean up everything in his cell to his satisfaction) but he, eventually, knocked on the wall to get my attention and handed me a cigarette that he had wrote "suck on this!" on and started laughing. We laughed and joked about these and many other things between us for years but they all came to an end April 26, 1994 when the state of Texas stuck a needle in his arm, pumped him full of drugs, and ended his existence. This Coke's for him!

Perry Williams
#999420

Age: 28
Hometown: Houston
Last school: Northshore High School, Houston; Tyler Junior College, Tyler
Education: Freshman in college
Interests: Reading, writing short stories/poems, sports, movies, and music
Favorites: *Book* - The Coldest Winter Ever; *Ice cream - Moollienum Crunch; Movie -* Belly; *Car - Lincoln Town Car*
Other info: I was raised a Christian but am really into all forms of religion, but have been settled on Islam, and love my family and friends, and love reading historical books such as The Prince by Machiavelli and Greek/Roman history.

Something to Live For

At times you may feel that you're damned if you do and damned if you don't, but you are truly mistaken. It's just that our expectations are unrealistic about how life should go for us as individuals. The only thing in life guaranteed for us as human beings is death and struggle while we do live. We will experience both good and bad, and yeah, for some of us, we may experience more bad than good in our lifetime. And most of the time, we do have some control over how much of the bad we go through, because some of the negative things we experience are a result of what we do and how we think. And how we think is reflected in what we do, how we live and how we respond to things.

We were all sent here to die, but all of us will not end up dying as a result of what we do. Some of us will, yet many of us won't. So, since we know that death could become our end, this whole experience is more about "how" we deal with the possibility and how we choose to live! If we allow death or its possibility to prevent us from extending our hands to others, then we have been defeated by something that is a natural part of our journey. There is nothing unnatural about death, nothing strange about it.

If we choose to crawl into a hole and turn away from others because they may die, then we are in violation because we have taken away the possibility that they have been put in our path in order to learn some valuable life's lessons from us. The lessons which may be intended for them to pass along to someone else. The chain would be broken and someone will be denied an important lesson, because of our selfishness.

Because of what we have gained from our friendships with others who have passed on, we are hopefully better people and a truer reflection of what it really means to be a brother, sister, friend! We are our brother's, sister's, friend's keeper and we should strive to be so and for those who are still here.

If I was selfish or did not love my people or all the forms of life as I say I do, then I would not be giving you this, and if I did not give you this, then I would have prevented your growth. And how do I know what it is you may eventually learn and gain from this? What I'm saying is this, it's not just about us as individuals, that it's about more than just us. And just as we had to depend on someone else to assist us in the past when we would not do for ourselves, we have an "obligation" to do the same for those who truly need and deserve our assistance.

So we have plenty to live for, obligations to still be fulfilled, and lessons yet to be learned. So we try, not simply for ourselves, but for others as well. For those who care about us and those who we care about. For those who still need us, such as your family and friends!!!!!

So stand true upon your square and live.

Open Eyes

When I was growing up, I guess you could say that I was one of those kids who was always getting into something. I was hard-headed, but honestly I really was not a bad kid. What I was, was basic. I was one of those people who had to go through things myself. It seems I refused to learn from the mistakes of others. Instead I went out and made my own mistakes. Stupid? Maybe in one sense, but I know without a doubt that learning lessons of life by going through a bad experience and making your own mistakes teaches you the first time. Rarely did I make the same mistakes twice.

It took me a long time to realize that it was a mistake to always have to go through things myself. Once I figured out that, life seemed to be a lot easier. But, it took being placed within my current predicament to open my eyes. With the realization that at times it is not best to make your own mistakes. I also learned that sometimes the lessons you learn from mistakes puts you in a position where you are stuck and then mistakes follow you to your grave.

I find myself in such a position. At the age of nineteen, I made the gravest mistake of my life and got directly involved with a robbery that cost a man his life. Now, eight years later, I sit on death row fighting to save my own life. All this because I refused to learn from the mistakes of others and insisted on going through everything myself. I learned my lesson and today I learn from what others have been through but this was a very hard lesson.

When I was growing up I was the baby of the family. I did not really have any older cousins that I was close to or who lived by me, so I found myself dealing with adults. In school I had some problems getting along with kids my age, because I was not used to dealing with them. I was used to dealing with adults. One would expect that by being around adults so much of the time I would have absorbed some of their wisdom and knowledge.

Well, I can't say that I learned nothing, but I admit to missing out on a lot of what could have made my life so much more less DRAMA-FILLED.

Once I realized that I needed to do my best to learn from the experiences of others, I was already in jail. But from day one I found myself drawn to the older cats. Of course I kicked it with dudes my age, but I noticed that I really vibed and sucked up all the older convicts had to teach me. I was in a new world, and I was not trying to learn hard lessons from personal experience. But unfortunately I did.

The first old school cat I ran into was a dude who had like twelve solid years in prison under his belt. Although he was only thirteen years my senior, he had prison experience, so I hung with him a lot and tried to learn as much as I could.

I was twenty-one when I came to death row, and the first friend I made here was a thirty year old man who had been locked up more years than he's been free. I guess you could say that in a sense I sat at his feet and absorbed everything I could. He is dead and gone now, but the lessons he taught me through our many talks still remain with me today.

Over the years I have gotten close with numerous "old timers." I saw something that I guess passed me by when I was free and that was that a person does not get to go through so many years of life and learn nothing. This was something that I did not see when I was free.

I thought that my parents were "out of tune with the times." I thought that "old people" were stuck in the past and really did not know what was going on with kids of that time. I thought that my parents and those few teachers who cared about me were just basically crazy or senile. Like so many youths I had the mentality that I knew it all or that at least I knew how to run my life better than anyone else. Boy was I wrong.

I see today that I missed out on so much because I did not take the time to really listen to what my elders said. Maybe if I had, had someone older that I was close to who was old enough to have experienced life, but young enough to relate to me I would not be where I am today. Maybe, if I would have opened my eyes to the fact that people don't get that much age under their belts by being stupid, I would have spared myself my greatest mistakes.

I can think about the "if's" all day, but that does not change the present. I can't change the past, but it is possible to touch someone out there who is not too far gone and make them realize what I did not. It is possible to use my life experiences to help someone avoid the mistakes I made on my own. It is possible to show someone that they don't have to do everything on their own.

I'm twenty-eight years old and in that time I have done a lot of living. I was sitting where many youth of today are sitting right now. I thought it was cool to get high, have crazy sex, sell dope and have money. I thought it was cool to dress fly and be popular. I thought it was cool to live it up. But then I saw that all of those thoughts were wrong. I realized that all things come in good time and that I should have enjoyed each step of life instead of trying to grow up so fast. I see now that all those so-called cool things in the end were not cool after all.

The same kids who smoked weed are now into heavier drugs and either locked up or halfway locked into a vicious cycle of addiction (whether physical or just psychological). Those same kids who had all the girls and were having the crazy sex either have some disease they can't give back or have kids they can't deal with or don't know what to do with. The same ones who sold drugs and had all the money and fly clothes are locked up with too many years to count. The list goes on and on.

Maybe these people are thinking just like me that they should have paid more attention to the mistakes of others. Maybe someone out there will read this and think twice about the life they are living and begin looking at the future and not just now and today. Maybe someone will re-evaluate their life based on these few words and make a change for the better before it is too late.

Then too it is possible that to some I'm just an old man who is out of touch with reality and not in tune with the times. For those, if I'm alive to see it, I'll see you somewhere in the prison population in about five or ten years or read about you in the obituaries someday not too far down the line. Or maybe I'll see you as a youngster on a death row just like I myself was in the beginning.

It's your life. Live it how you please. I just hope that someone, at least one person out there, takes heed to these words and makes some changes to prevent them from following in my footsteps and the stage of many young people locked up today.

Peace, love, and respect,
Perry E. Williams Jr.

Robert Woodard
#999388

Age: 28
Education: *Eleventh grade*

Grown Man Cry

Tell me, is it alright for a grown man to cry? Tears spark in the dark from the wells of my eyes. It's like that when trying to stay strong in a world you truly despise, it's like that when searching the depths of your soul where your true feelings lie. Hard and harder to maintain these years feeling deranged, the pressure to stabilize a discipline fashion the tears the pain. With deception and deceit my foes consistently look for defeat, still remains death before dishonor I sustain.

Tears flow from the hurt like raindrops that nourish the dirt, feeding to the need to release the anger before destruction occurs. To advert from the frustration, the madness, the rage, let the feelings disperse, comes forth a plant of peace that lurks through the mist of the murk. My sentiments are to never emerge, but like a curse they pour. From the depths of my soul with psychotic episodes, my sanity I attempt to hold. Since my thoughts are trapped in a code of silence, these tears are the only way for my story to ever be told.

Christopher Young
#999508

Age: 25
Hometown: San Antonio
Last school: Roosevelt High School, San Antonio
Education: Nine and a half
Interests: Reading and writing poetry, fighting to end the death penalty and all injustice across the world
Favorites: I love to play chess. The competitiveness and strategies can assist us in everyday life. I also love to study U.S. and world history.
Other info: I'm also a part of a prison activist group that fights the death penalty from the inside, Death Row Inner-Communalist Vanguard Engagement (DRIVE). We also assist in fighting numerous social struggles and injustices across America and throughout the world. We do this through non-violent, direct action.

The Editors

Dana Allen received her MA degree in English from Sam Houston State University and holds a BA in English and journalism from East Texas State University. She is working toward her MFA in creative writing at San Jose State University and plans to pursue a career teaching English at the college level.

Regina Bouley has received a BA in English from Sam Houston State University and has completed an MA in the same field. Her short term goal is to teach at the community college level. She loves words because they hold ideas.

Paula Khalaf has completed an MA in English at Sam Houston State University. She holds a Master of Education in curriculum and instruction and a BA in philosophy, both from University of Houston. She is currently associate professor of transitional studies at Lone Star College-CyFair in Cypress, Texas.

James Ridgway recently completed a BA in philosophy at the University of Houston–Downtown. Unfortunately, the philosophy factory was not currently hiring, so he joined Sam Houston State University's English MA program.

Haley Stoner holds a BA in English and an MA in theological studies. She is currently pursuing an MA in English at Sam Houston State University and plans to continue on in academia. Eventually, she hopes to teach college students full time in the disciplines of English and ethics.

Daniel Stryker earned a BS and an MA in history from Sam Houston State University as well as an MA in education and an Ed.D from the University of Houston. He has taught high school history and has taught college history for 11 years. While his academic focus is primarily history, he would love the opportunity to also teach English.

Cami Whitehead attained a BA in English and a MA in communication studies from Texas Tech University. She is currently completing an MA in English from Sam Houston State University and is pursuing a career in technical editing.